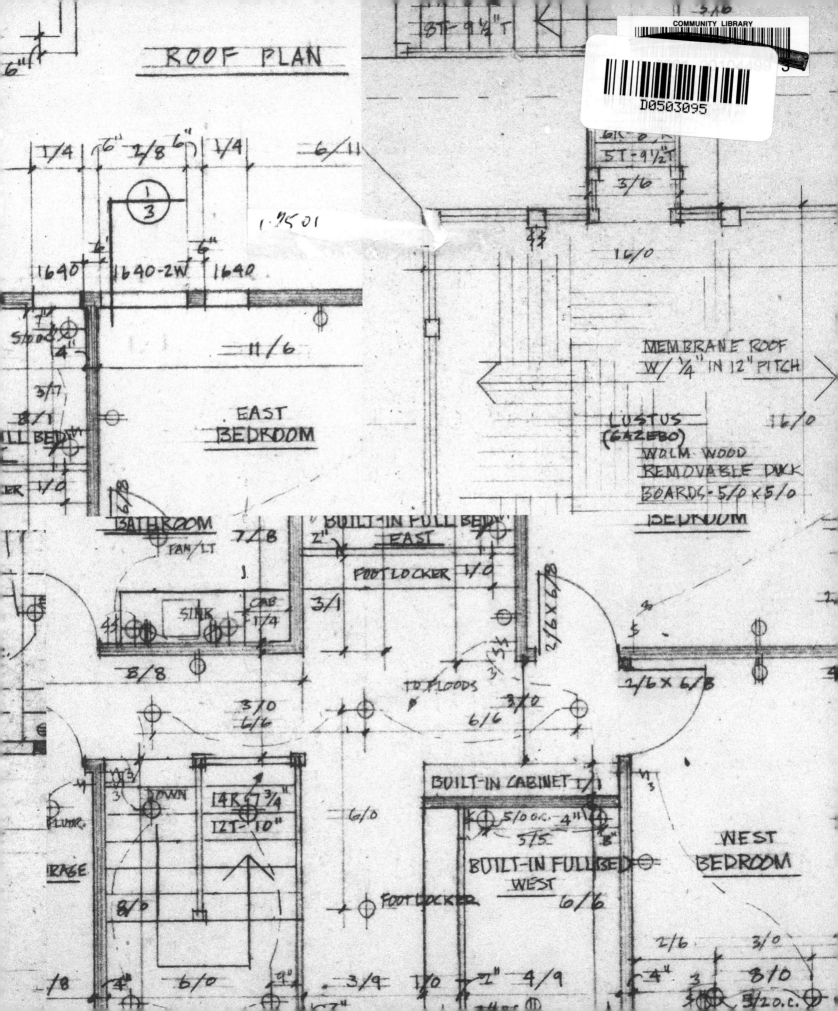

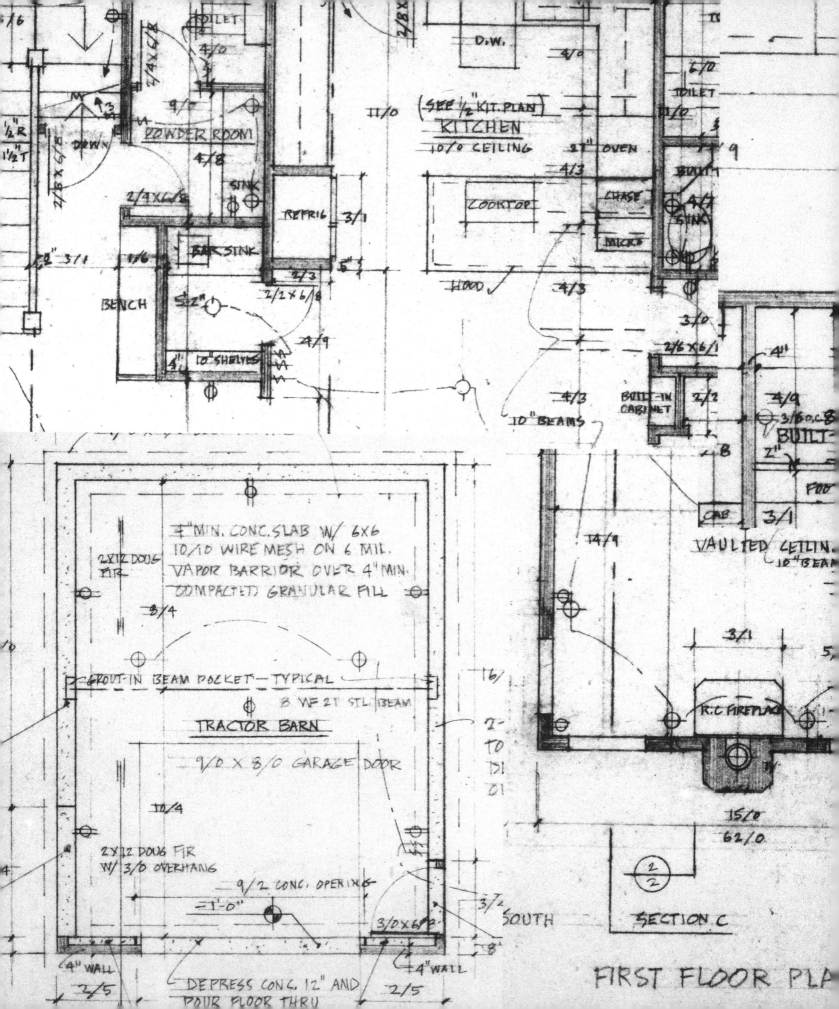

Country Living

FOREWORD BY
RACHEL NEWMAN

PRODUCED BY
NANCY MERNIT SORIANO

COUNTRY BY DESIGN
THE SCANDI

PHOTOGRAPHS BY
KEITH SCOTT MORTON

TEXT BY
MARY SEEHAFER SEARS

NAVIAN LOOK

HEARST BOOKS · NEW YORK

Library of Congress Cataloging-In-Publication Data

The Scandinavian look: country by design / Country living
photographs by Keith Scott Morton : text by Mary Seehafer Sears.
1st ed.
    p.   cm.
ISBN 0-688-15096-9
1. Country homes--Wisconsin. 2. Decoration and ornament, Rustic-
-Scandinavia--Influence. 3. Interior decoration--Scandinavia-
-Influence.   I. Sears, Mary Seehafer. II. Morton, Keith Scott.
III. Country living (New York, N.Y.)
NA7561.S33   1997
728'.37'09775--dc21

Printed in Singapore

FOR COUNTRY LIVING

Rachel Newman *Editor-in-Chief*

Nancy Mernit Soriano, *Executive Editor*

Julio Vega, *Art Director*

John Mack Carter, *President, Hearst Magazine Enterprises*

FIRST EDITION

1 2 3 4 5 6 7 8 9 10

Editor: Gail Kinn
Designer: Susi Oberhelman
Illustrator: Lou Heiser
Floor Plans Illustrated by: Muriel Cuttrell

Carl Larsson images courtesy of The American Swedish Institute

PRODUCED BY SMALLWOOD & STEWART, INC., NEW YORK CITY

IN   THIS   WORLD...

CONTENTS

Several years ago, a beautiful set of watercolor renderings appeared in my office. They were an architect's conceptualization of a Scandinavian homestead—a main house and several outbuildings that would be built in Wisconsin. I immediately thought of Carl Larsson's home in Sweden and

my magical visit there ten years ago. I literally ran into executive editor Nancy Soriano's office, renderings in hand, and we both knew instantly that we must bring this project to the pages of *Country Living*. The size and scale of this undertaking were larger than anything we had done in the past, but Nancy accepted the challenge with gusto, and agreed to shepherd the project through the stages of building, furnishing, and photography. When finished we realized it was a story that would go way beyond a single issue, that it warranted its own book. We hope you enjoy this wonderful home.

RACHEL NEWMAN Editor-in-Chief, Country Living Magazine

In these pages you'll witness the design, construction, and decoration of a unique, once-in-a lifetime home—an inspiration to the eye and to the soul. Here a homeowner's dream is realized by a designer's vision. Their collaboration demonstrates how necessity and talent can be combined to great ends. Designer Lou Heiser has found the perfect balance of color and scale, and made it all easy to live with; homeowner Loran Nordgren trusted both Lou and himself sufficiently to follow the spirit of the design. As for me, this was one of the most exciting projects with which I have been involved.

NANCY MERNIT SORIANO Executive Editor, Country Living Magazine

My parents were born in Wisconsin, and I like to lie and say I was

born there too. I spent most of my childhood weekends bound for

America's Dairyland, our musty green canvas tent and plaid-lined

sleeping bags strapped

to the top of the family Ford as we shuttled from my hometown

of Northbrook, Illinois, to places like Green Lake, Madison, Devil's

Lake, Wisconsin Rapids, and DeForest. So when *Country Living* asked

me to write this book, it was like coming home. Everyone I spoke to

sounded like a relative, with their wonderful Midwestern voices

and friendly ways; they brought back lots of memories. ■ I'd like to

introduce you to them: The homeowner, Loran Nordgren, is a noble

man with a noble vision, who cares deeply for his family, and for the

land. He is a wonderful storyteller. He has accomplished something

most of us can only dream of, and turned a vision into a splendid reality. We thank him for letting us into his world. ■ The designer, Lou Heiser, has a red truck called Old Blue and he loves Sumatran coffee. Lou was more than generous with his time and expertise. One of Lou's favorite expressions in talking about the people on the project was, "They brought something to the party." His talents certainly led the way. I'm awestruck by his brilliance and am touched by his kind heart. ■ I've learned much from Lou. If you're trying to decide between 4-inch posts and 6-inch posts, choose the 6-inch posts; in design, bigger always looks better. If an idea comes, park it; you'll use it someday. The more glass the merrier. Two tablespoons coffee to six ounces water. ■ Lou told me this joke, courtesy of comedian Michael Feldman on Wisconsin Public Radio: In Wisconsin, you need two coats: a parka and a dress parka. ■ Next time I visit, I'm bringing both! MARY SEEHAFER SEARS

PART ONE

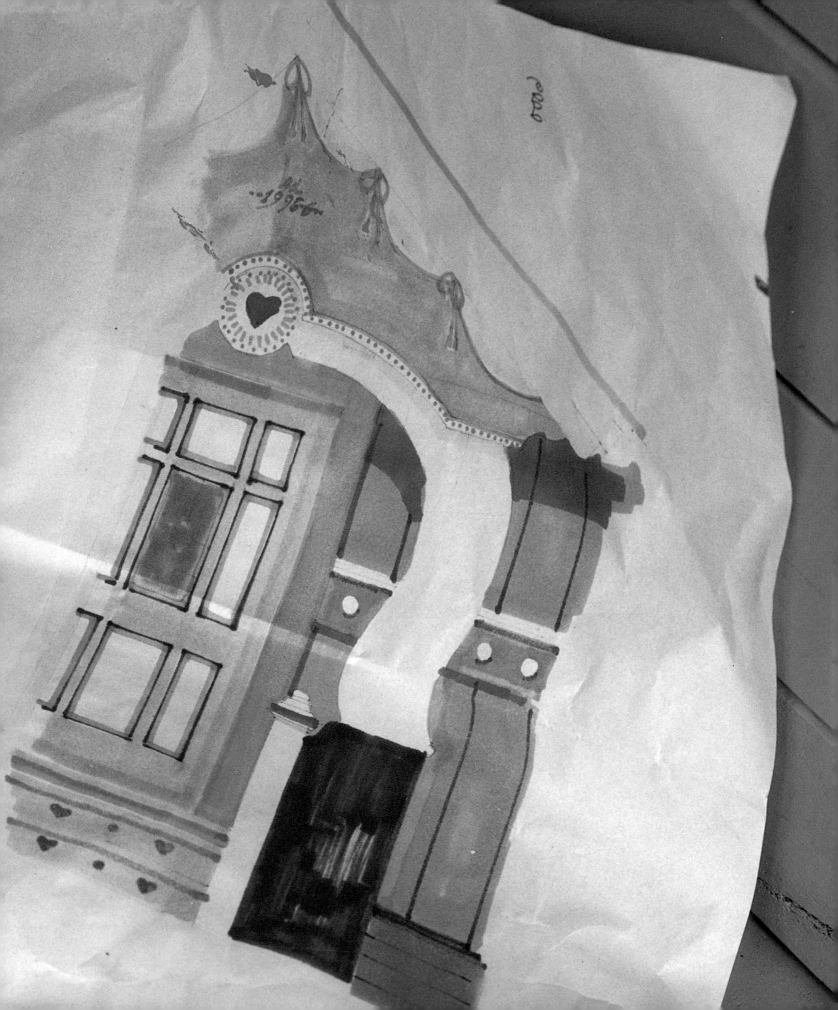

Where do ideas come from? How do you transform a dream into a reality? During a trip to Sweden, Loran Nordgren was so **THE IDEA** moved by the story-book home of 19th-century artist Carl Larsson that it re-awakened his 20-year-long dream of building a spacious family complex. He wanted a place where his children and grandchildren could gather; a place with rooms that would bring family together but which would also allow

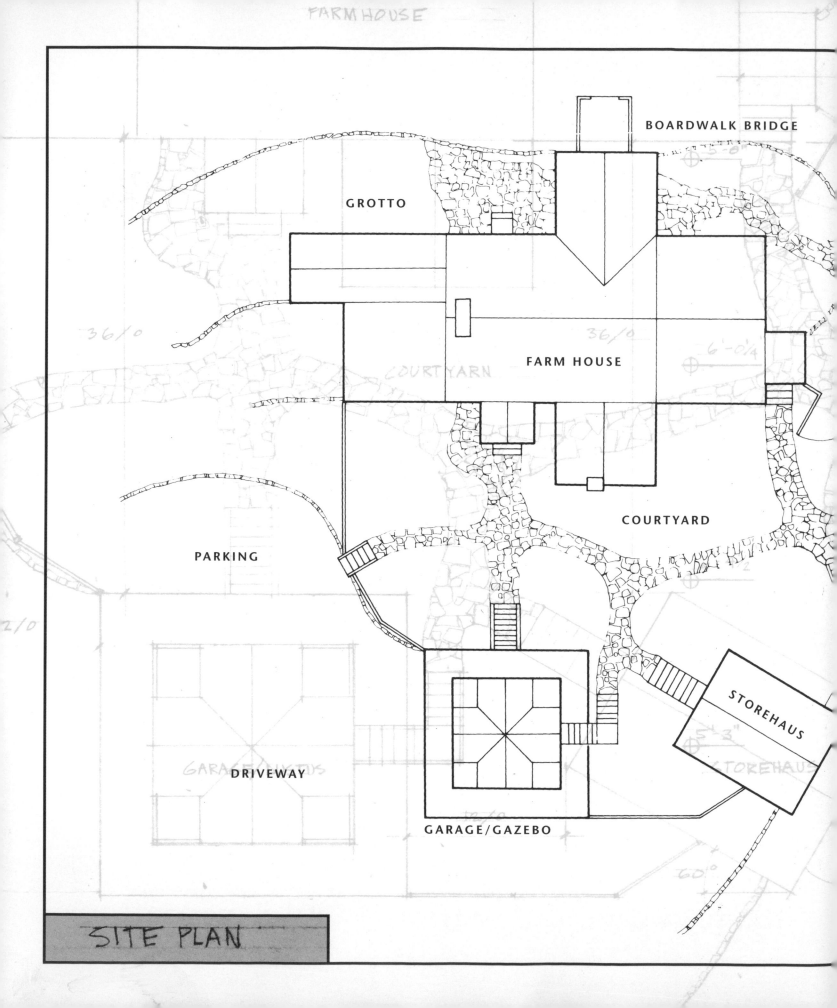

FARMHOUSE

BOARDWALK BRIDGE

GROTTO

FARM HOUSE

COURTYARD

PARKING

COURTYARD

DRIVEWAY

GARAGE/GAZEBO

STOREHAUS

SITE PLAN

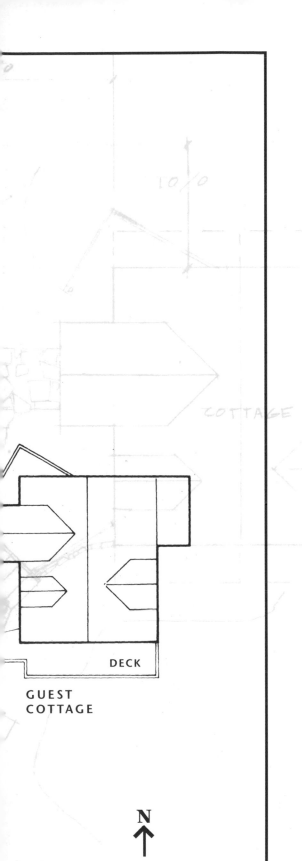

GUEST
COTTAGE

DECK

N

0   5   10FT

for solitude. And he had just the right setting: 420 acres in southwestern Wisconsin, graced with the same dense green forests, bright blue skies, and clear light that had delighted him in Sweden.

It wasn't Loran Nordgren's first trip to Sweden; he'd been there twice before. But this was the first time he'd visited Dalarna, the province of his ancestors. Well-known for its literary and artistic heritage, Dalarna is typically Swedish. On summer Sundays, folks still dress in peasant costume and row across the lake to church in huge boats that hold 20 or 30 people. Dalarna is famous for its picturesque beauty, its August crayfish festivals, and its itinerant painters of the past, who originated a unique style of sprightly wall decorations. Perhaps most importantly, Dalarna was home to Carl Larsson, one of Sweden's most cherished artists of the

A bird's-eye view of the compound is shown in the blueprint (opposite), with all four buildings clustered around a central courtyard, the *storehaus* in the south-east corner offsetting the symmetry. There is a stone grotto area behind the main house, and flagstone walkways join the buildings, which sit on a terraced slope surrounded by rock walls; most of the stone was culled from the property. The pond and one of Nordgren's two landing strips lie to the south.

Silhouetted against the sky, a majestic carved eagle guards the house (above), just as wooden roof carvings fend off evil spirits on old Scandinavian churches and buildings. The eagle also appears in the Nordgren family crest. The cottage (opposite) is protected by a dragon, a prominent symbol in early Scandinavian woodworking. From the driveway, stairs lead up to the compound, its village-like aspect well in evidence (previous page). Nordgren flies the flags of the United States, Sweden, and Norway high on the hill behind his house, in salute to his neighbors and all those who worked on the house (overleaf). The flag lines run inside the 35- and 40-foot fiber-glass staffs, which were specially ordered from Sweden.

late 19th century. He settled with his wife Karin and seven children in a farmhouse inherited from his father-in-law in the tiny town of Sundborn.

Charmed by Dalarna, Nordgren headed for the Larsson farmhouse, hoping he could just look around. He was delighted to discover that the house was now a museum and he could freely roam the compound—which he did for several hours. The place felt lived in and cherished. He could imagine how a family had grown and thrived there; the farmhouse rambled, with additions tacked on as the Larssons became more prosperous over the years. Looking at it all, Nordgren saw parallels with his own life. With six children and eleven grandchildren scattered around the country, he longed to establish a place where the family could gather at any time of the year. The design and spirit of the Larsson complex inspired Nordgren, and he believed he could re-create its charm and beauty back home in Wisconsin. Twenty years earlier, Nordgren had bought a parcel of land in Wisconsin intending to build on it someday. Over the years he'd camped and hiked on the land with his family, but somehow the dream of building a home never crystallized—until this trip to Sweden. Once he'd

seen the Larsson home, he knew exactly what he wanted. He would construct a complex loosely based on the Larsson farmhouse.

Back home in Chicago, Nordgren was fired up. There was only one problem: he lived five hours from the Wisconsin site, and was so busy with work he could hardly imagine administering so demanding a construction project. Who could design his dream house?

Coincidentally, soon after he returned from Sweden, Nordgren heard that a business acquaintance, Lou Heiser, had moved to Wisconsin, not far from his property. As the owner of a marketing and advertising agency, Nordgren had frequently sought the services of Heiser's design company.

Heiser is an artist and award-winning illustrator who had studied architecture, and seemed the perfect person for the job. The two men met for lunch and a deal was sealed.

"I always feel I'm fifty percent designer, fifty percent psychologist," laughs Heiser while talking about the process of getting inside a client's head. "An architect needs to see where his client lives, to get a sense of the person, his tastes, and his temperament." The next step was a visit to Nordgren's current home, a large modern house in the woods.

For Nordgren tall ceilings, wide windows and an open flow of space were paramount. Nordgren described his hopes for a lively family homestead and gave Heiser books and postcards of what he'd seen in Sweden. "I want to build a house like Larsson's," Nordgren told Heiser. "It was an inspiration—but my intention is not to duplicate Carl Larsson's farmhouse, but to interpret it for my own family. The ceilings there are often just seven feet high, the rooms are small, and there aren't many views; still, I want to work in that idiom."

Inspired, Heiser retreated to his studio and the ideas began to flow. ∎

Many details in the house were taken directly from Lilla Hyttnäs, Carl Larsson's house in Sweden. Larsson had a lettered frieze on his studio walls—the same idea was adapted for the family room (opposite) using the Nordgren children's names.

Automotive striping tape created straight–line borders. A red bookshelf similar to this one appears in Carl Larsson's bedroom. Over a doorway at the far end of the room (overleaf) is a dinner–prayer found on a Swedish placemat, chosen because, frankly, it fit nicely into the space.

In Jesu nam
Välsigna Gu

Till bords vi gå.
Den mat vi få.
nen.

ARTE ET PROBITATE

1897

CARL LARSSON

Carl Larsson (1853–1919) is one of Sweden's most beloved painters. Many of his paintings share irresistible images of family life at Lilla Hyttnäs, the home where he and his wife, Karin, raised their seven children. The house was a marvel to his fellow Swedes because of its lighthearted atmosphere; most of the country was mired in a heavy dark decorating style that the Larssons helped sweep away. Both Carl and Karin were artists, and fell in love at an artists' colony in France.

The Larssons' Swedish farmhouse in Sundborn, in the province of Dalarna, was inherited from Karin's father, and was previously occupied by her grandmother and two elderly aunts. What a change when the Larsson family invaded the property! Soon there were costume parades, fishing in the creek by the house, meals outside under the birch trees, and a general air of merriment. As in any family, there were good days and bad. *A Late-Riser's Miserable Breakfast* depicts a woeful morning for the painter's daughter Kersti (left). Larsson's allegorical mural, *Outdoors Blow the Summer Winds* (below), depicts the renewal of life in story form. How faithful Larsson's idyllic paintings were to his actual life will really never be known; like all families, the Larssons projected an image to the world that Sweden still holds true.

The house took on many additions over the

years as the Larsson family grew and became more prosperous. The small farmhouse, with its maze of rooms, began to ramble here and there. Larsson attached a large sunny studio with a high ceiling that became not only his workroom, but a family living room and a place for parties. Karin was a weaver and textile artist who designed linens, tapestries, and furniture for the house in her signature style, colorful and simple, and dressed herself and her children in unique fashions. Karin probably had just as great an influence on the look of their house as Larsson did, and together they worked side by side to create a beautiful place to live; *Lazy Nook* (right) is a famous look at their airy drawing room. Portraits of the family and oversized lettering decorate the walls, which Larsson sectioned off with moldings and paint so that they could be freely written and painted upon. Truly, their house was their canvas.

Today the Larsson home is a museum, and hosts thousands of visitors annually. But the Larsson family still visits several times a year. When they arrive, the house is closed to the public and Carl Larsson's descendants once again sleep in the beds, cook on the stoves, and scamper beneath the birches, fulfilling the family motto: "Let it remain a living home." ■

PART TWO

RAILING CAP
RAILING W/CUT-OUTS
6×6 POST
EXISTING 6×6
DOUBLE 1×12

5115A

8201

4815A

NEW
LATEX

8611W
Rainforest Dew

8183W
Candlebark
CGI

3'-3"   3'-3"

PG. 10

A Scandinavian house rarely stands alone. Typically, several structures cluster together around a central courtyard; as **THE DESIGN** on the old Scandinavian farm, where a house was paired with a barn, and often a *storehaus* or *stabur*, a Norwegian outbuilding for guests. This complex became a kind of village, serving not only as a family compound but also providing protection from the elements. Heiser describes the

COLOR TO COME

FRONT ENTRANCE

5563

5114

4705

F 82

ENT. CLOSET
OUTSIDE
(INSIDE-SOLID)

F 82

POWDER RM
- 2- SIDES

OUTS

4275

8045

CABOTS
LT. GREEN
ACRYLIC

BATH

BASEMENT STOR.

BALCONY & DECK
OUTSIDE

BALCON
INSID

5563
5115
4275

TAUX MARBLE

8201
8045
4275

RAG

2ND FL. BATH
2-SIDES

8615
8503

EAST BEDRM
2-SIDES

WEST BEDRM
2-SIDES

5565

design process as a juggling of many influences. "Before you've even begun," he explains, "you've read books, visited museums, and photographed interesting elements. The arched detail on Nordgren's second-floor siding was something I saw on a Victorian facade at Disney World 25 years ago." By the time Heiser began doodling he could already see the compound in his mind's eye.

The basic scheme unfolded on his floor plan: a rambling house with many wings. "I designed a shed roof, accentuated by a severe wall," recalls Heiser, "to create Nordgren's tall living room. I drew a narrow section—the balcony over the living room—leading to the second-floor loft overlooking the pond, and a crow's nest to top off the third

floor. The more dormers and shapes we added, the more interesting the house became."

In quick succession there appeared a two-story cottage for children and grandchildren, a garage crowned by an open-air gazebo, and, to complete the quadrangle, the rustic sod-roofed *storehaus*, set at an angle and built into the hillside.

The steel roofing chosen for the house, cottage, and garage–gazebo mimics the Scandinavian S-tile roof. Its durability makes it particularly well-suited to snow, and its drum-like surface makes a symphony out of a storm.

Although Heiser assumed the house would be red, as is common in Scandinavia, he was concerned it would become lost among the red Wisconsin barns. When Nordgren came across a photograph of a Scandinavian house painted a mustard color, he chose that instead, and a stain was specially matched.

"The Scandinavian aspects of the compound are more a matter of details than layout," explains Heiser, ". . . the pitch of the roofs, the eagle and dragon carvings, the decorative painting."

Now that the house was designed, the next question rose up: where to put it? ■

Heiser finds that colored sketches are a quick way to see how various color combinations work together. Rather than painting an actual surface, he first experiments with markers, testing out different color combinations and judging their effect. He gave the painters his drawings, specifying colors and details; then he let them fly with their own inspirations, with marvelous results. The sketches (opposite) were ideas for matching paneled doors in the foyer of the house. The white plaster animal panels set into the doors were glazed to look old. The sketches (previous page) contain ideas for other doors throughout the compound.

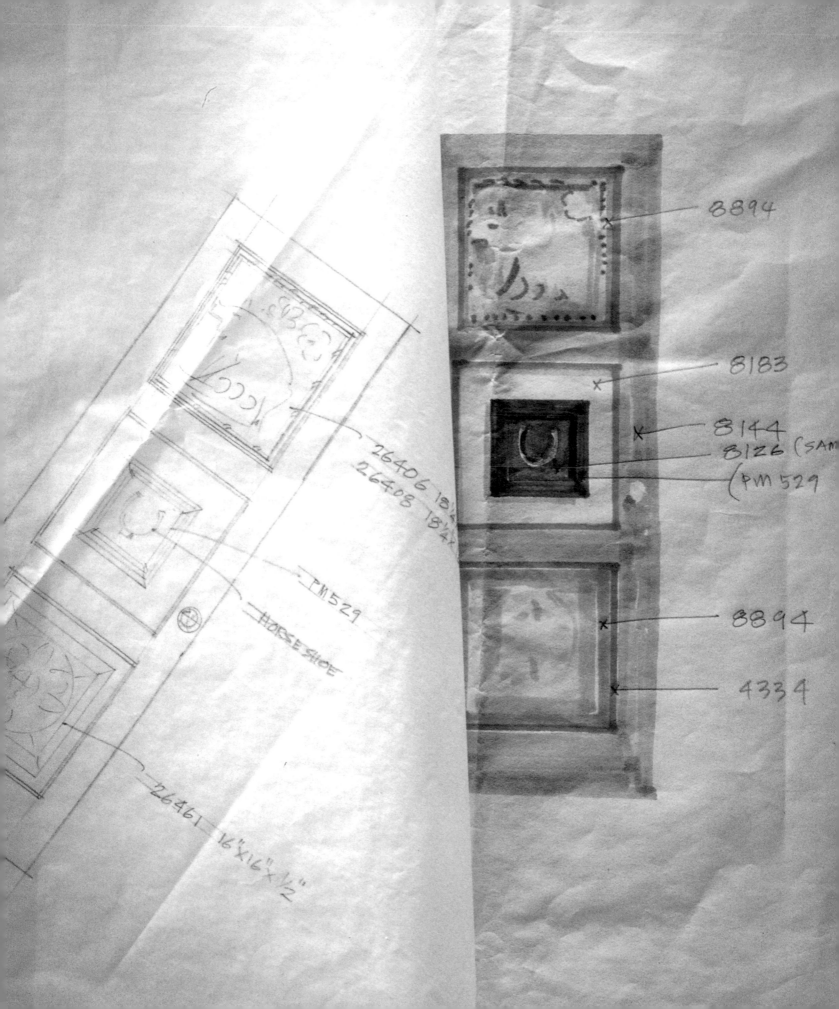

8894

8183

8144
8126 (SAM
(PM 529

8894

4334

26406 18¼
26408 18½

PM529

HORSESHOE

26461   16"x16"x½

WEST

VIEWING LOFT

SOUTH NORTH

NORTH

STUGA/KITCHEN

PLASTER WALLS

WOOD WALLS

WINDOWS/TRIM

SHELF UNITS

SHELF BACKS

NORTH SOUTH

2ND FLOOR

BUILT-IN

HALL STRIPES

HALL STRIPES

WAINSCOTE

TRIM

BUILT-IN

EAST WEST

BUILT-IN FULL

BUILT-IN TWIN (OVER BUT.)

1ST FLOOR LIVING RM/DINING

WALLS

BEAMS/UNDERS

COTTAGE

NORTH EAST

SOUTH WEST

E25

CEILING

E24

UPPER WALLS

F23

LOWER WALLS

8144M
Revere Green

RAILINGS/
TRIM

WINDOWS/TRIM

LIVING ROOM

THE PAINT PALETTE

The Nordgren house is decorated in soft Gustavian colors, while bright saturated shades hold forth in the cottage. Both palettes are typical of Scandinavia, the Gustavian palette being the more formal of the two.

The advent of Gustavian style brought light and air into Scandinavian homes, replacing the heavy Rococo look of the mid-18th century with white ceilings, pale floors, simple window treatments, and an emphasis on painted wall decoration. The color palette reflects the flowering of Swedish culture during the 18th century, when King Gustav the Third (1742–1792), a worldly ruler who loved to travel, brought the cosmopolitan ideas of Germany to his native land.

Homemade Scandinavian paints included oil paints made of dry pigments and oil; distemper made of dry pigments, chalk, water, and animal glue (size); and limewash, a lime-and-water mixture sometimes tinted with pigment. These paint colors mellow and darken with time; some old finishes have lasted for centuries.

For the Nordgren house, Heiser chose from a fan deck of latex (water-based) paints, clipping swatches to color cards for painters Dan Tagtmeyer and Harry Adams to work from. There were so many colors in the house that the three of them conversed in a shorthand of paint numbers: "Do that in 8114." Each can was numbered on the bottom in case the tops got switched. The paints were of such good quality and the colors so well chosen that decorative painter Sandra Russell sometimes used them as artist's colors, thinned with water and applied directly to the walls like distemper. The paints merged with the surface, and selective sanding aged them a bit, until they took on a velvety look. Sandra also created her own washes by mixing artist's colors with the white paint used on all the walls.

Heiser advises choosing a paddle book with appealing shades in the color range you're looking for; custom mixing breaks the formula and allows for error if you need to mix more paint. Heiser also suggests buying a quart and painting a wall before you do a whole house or a whole room, and he speaks from experience: it took three test quarts to get a correct color for the entryway of the house. But it was well worth the testing. ■

SOUTH ELEVATION

WEST E

ON

ENTRANCE DETAIL

LOFT PIT   SCALE ½"=1'-0"

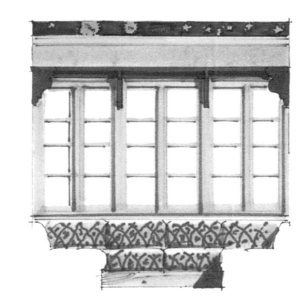

ENTRY ■━━━━━━━━━━━━━━━━━━━━━━━━ ■ SCALE ½"=1'-0"

EAST ELEVATION

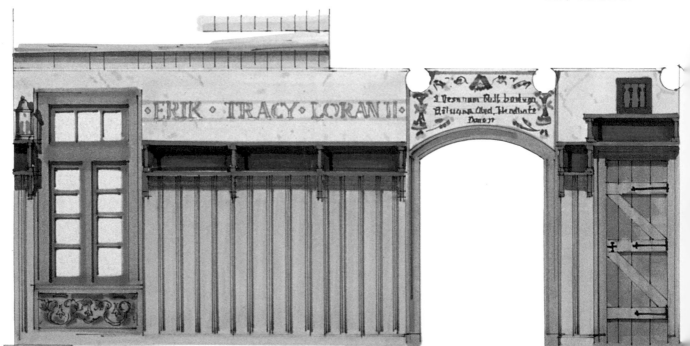

WEST ELEVATION

SOUTH ELEVATION

NORTH VAULT

STUGA   SCALE 1/2" = 1'-0"

NORTH ELEVATION

KITCHEN

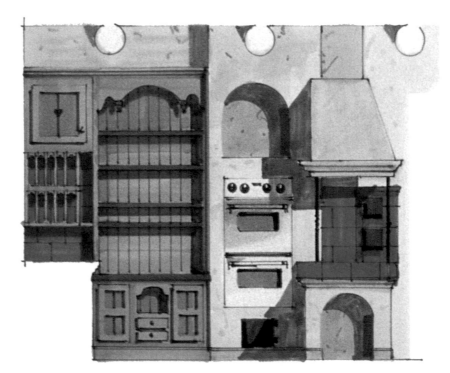

EAST ELEVATION

WEST ELEVATION

SCALE $\frac{1}{2}$" = 1'-0"

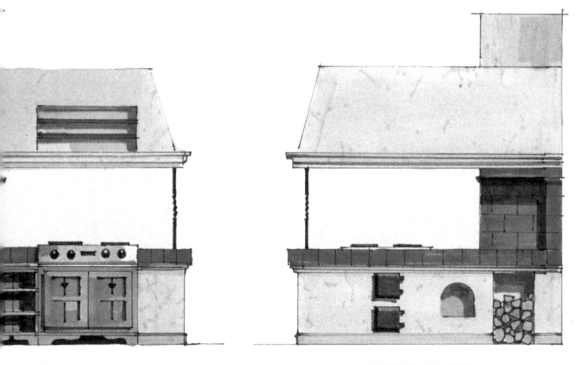

SOUTH ISLAND   NORTH ISLAND

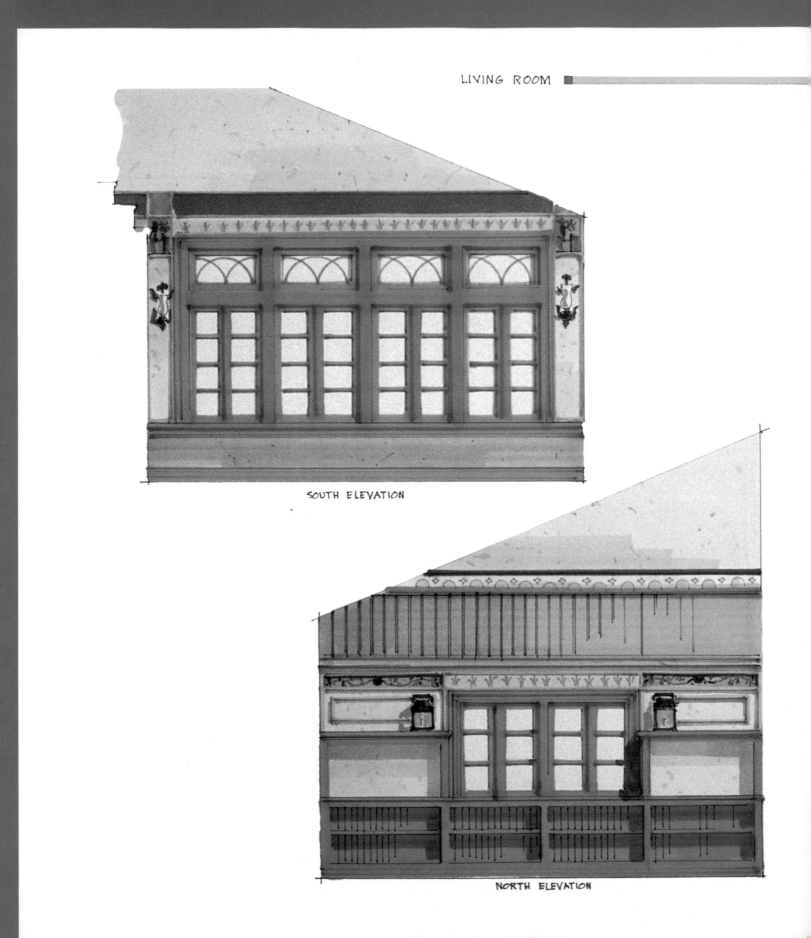

SOUTH ELEVATION

NORTH ELEVATION

SCALE ½" = 1'-0"

WEST ELEVATION

EAST ELEVATION

GUEST COTTAGE

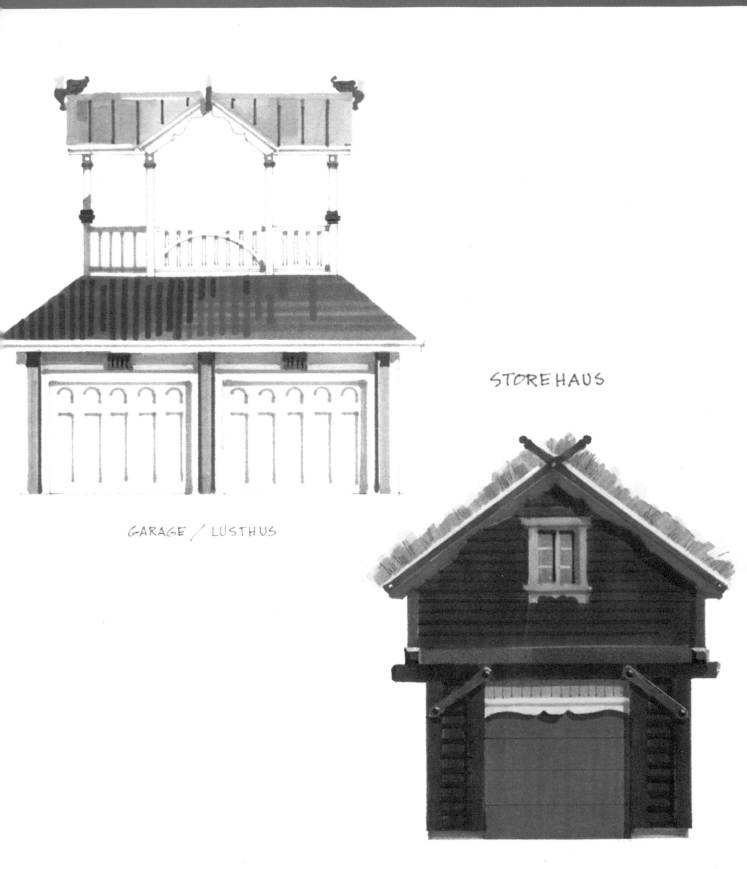

GARAGE / LUSTHUS

STOREHAUS

PART THREE

Siting a house is a subtle and sensitive process, where practical needs confront the land's mysteries. The task is to find a place where a house can sit solid and stand proud, as well as offer shelter and peace. In the end, what feels right may make sound design sense as well. Nordgren took a walk of the land by himself, looking for just such a site. His search led him to a spot between ridge and valley,

a half-mile from the main road with a splendid view of three ponds. Independently, Heiser chose the same site.

Heiser recalls his walk around the acreage. "A river flows through the valley here; I followed an abandoned grass farm road that echoes its path, looking for sun. If you have 420 acres, 300 of which are woods, you don't have to build among the trees," reasoned Heiser. "People always build their first house in the woods, but Nordgren had already done that." He wanted a site with an east–west axis; in the Midwest, it's ideal for the long part of a building to head east and west because of the pre-

vailing winds. There's a dam at one end of the property, sealing off a lake, so Heiser made certain the site was above the 100-year flood plain.

Parts of the house are truly from the land. No trees had to be cleared from this pastured slope to

American basswood trees, from the linden family, are abundant on the Nordgren property. Thirty tall, straight basswood were cut to make floorboards and stair treads for the house and cottage. Logger Randy Dalberg can determine how many board-feet a tree will pro-

vide just by looking at it, so no trees were cut unnecessarily (opposite). A log skidder drags the chain-wrapped logs down the hill (above); winter's frozen slopes promoted the process. On flat ground, the logs were cut into lengths and loaded onto a truck bound for the sawmill.

The logs were rough-sawn by Jack Bolden at the sawmill (left), then moved next door to the lumberyard for air-drying, kiln-drying, shaping and cutting. To speed up the drying process, little pieces of wood, called stickers, were placed between the boards as they were stacked, allowing air to circulate. The lumberyard also shaped poplar into the interior trim used throughout the house.

lay the foundations. But native American basswood trees were cut and milled to make random- width floorboards, and a single cherry tree was felled for countertops, stair railings, and shelves.

Building never obeys a schedule, and this project was no exception. Interior work began once the house was "under roof," which in this case was temporary, as first clay tile and then concrete tile were considered and rejected. In the meantime, the plywood roof was topped by a rubber membrane and extra-strong tar paper, which was reinforced several times to keep out snow and rain, until the steel roof was eventually laid.

With four separate buildings to construct, the hand-craftsmanship involved, and the difficulties

As winter progressed, the push was on to get the buildings "under roof," as they say in the building trade, allowing work to continue indoors during the coldest months. At this stage, both the house and neighboring cottage had plywood exterior walls, windows, and temporary plywood and tar paper roofs in place. Sheathing the buildings with a breathable protective shell of woven polyethylene-based fabric, called housewrap, blocked out the wind without trapping interior moisture. A bulldozer carved out the driveway during excavation of the foundation; a rock wall eventually stabilized the embankment.

in choosing a suitable roof, it took two and a half years to complete the compound. Heiser is no fan of traditional landscaping, so Scandinavian-style rock walls, walkways, and steps accent the house. "A well-designed house doesn't need foundation plantings," he maintains. Instead, these buildings hug the ground, their perimeters carefully planned. Several times rock appeared just where it was needed. Heiser had ordered flagstone for a patio behind the kitchen, and cement piers were to be poured to support the second floor study, but a flat stretch of limestone in that area eliminated the need for either. The only purchased stone was driveway gravel and the courtyard's Bryan red rock.

The layout quickly asserted itself once interior work began. A key structural element in the house is the fireplace (opposite). Its massive plywood shell is a chase for a 16-inch chimney pipe, duct work, low-voltage wiring, and 6 x 6 vertical timbers that stand on the foundation wall and soar skyward, supporting the living room roof beams and upper stories. On the backside of the chimney, decorative grilles disguise cold-air returns that circulate heated air through the house. Stairs behind the fireplace lead to the viewing loft, second-floor bedroom and study, and continue, out of sight, to the third floor.

THE PROCESS

Clear the site

Excavate the foundations

Pour foundation footings

Build foundation walls

Backfill and rough grading

Put in septic system and well

Frame the buildings

Put on the roofs

Weatherize the exteriors

Install fireplaces

Install and finish drywall

Install electric service, phone lines, rough plumbing, rough electric, and HVAC (heating, ventilation, air conditioning)

Pour basement and garage floors

Insulate

Install gutters and garage doors

Paint and/or stain the exterior

Install wall and floor tile

Put up trim

Paint the interior

Install kitchen and bath cabinets and plumbing fixtures

Finish plumbing, electric, and HVAC installation

Install and finish hardwood floors

Install appliances

Grade and landscape

Touch up paint

Final inspection

Certificate of Occupancy

As the project ended, a truckload of gravel was brought in to top-dress the driveway (opposite). Landscaping around the house is minimal, but a few plants were set into the slopes above the driveway to soften the terrain. Stairs lead down to the garage service door.

A man-made waterfall, reminiscent of Scandinavian terrain, cascades through two small collecting pools (above) before spilling into the pond to supply extra oxygen to the trout. A rock wall not only hides the foundation (right) but acts as a natural planter.

Drains in the planter carry water from low spots behind the house to below-ground drain tiles. Circular cut-outs in the porch skirt encourage air to circulate, protecting the wood floor from rot. Amazingly, the stone patio in the foreground is natural and reasonably level.

Local artisans embellished the cottage with warmth and personality. Bridget Gallagher gave a finishing touch to a closet door in the entry of the cottage (above left). Using her hand as a level, Sandra Russell decorated the recessed nook above the kitchen stove with an exuberant urn of flowers (above right). Her tools include water-based paints, an array of fine-bristle brushes, and buckets of talent. Wisconsin is famous for bright dry summer days, which are perfect for painting. The front door and posts of the cottage's covered entryway were treated to a coat of cheerful crabapple-green painted by Harry Adams (opposite left); this was the cottage's "neutral" color for

most of the moldings and trim.
Depressing the floor two inches
allowed room for the bluestone
floor that will soon be installed.
Three-quarters of the way through
the project, the built-in beds in the
upstairs hallway were framed out

and partly painted by Craig
Erickson (above right), while Al
Verbsky paints the stair surround,
made of narrow beaded paneling,
continuing the casual feeling of
the cottage. Experimenting with
different ways to lay wood

paneling on the walls, Heiser drew
the herringbone pattern for the
far wall, running upper boards
parallel with the roofline; painting
the boards in alternating colors
emphasizes the design.

PAINTING EXTERIORS

The outside of a Scandinavian home is a clue to what's inside. A modest house has a modest entrance; a fancier dwelling deserves an entrance with more stature. When the Nordgren house was first designed on paper, Heiser drew a plain covered entry with benches and open posts running along each side, much like the entrance on the back of the house. However, as the dwelling evolved, Nordgren asked for a more formal entrance in keeping with the rest of the house. By this time, the roof of the entrance was finished, and the 6 x 6 treated posts were in place, but there was still time to modify the look before it was enclosed and decorated. Heiser went back to the drawing board, eliminating the original yellow door in favor of a paneled door on which he could mount Nordgren's Irish doorknocker. The curved supports, center medallion with Nordgren's initials, and scalloped bargeboards with swag-and-bow motifs were adapted from the entrance of a rustic farmhouse in the northern Swedish province of Hälsingland.

Until the mid-1800s, Swedish timbered houses were usually unpainted. Then the ubiquitous Falun red began to dominate the landscape. This color was made of oxides from the copper mines in the town of Falun in Dalarna, and was inexpensive and readily available. Painting your house another color—a limewash of ochre, soft pink, or orange—identified you as someone who could afford the better things in life. All the colors were chosen to stand out against winter's snowy white and the leafy greens of springtime.

The Nordgren house is sheathed with 1 x 12 Western red cedar batten-board siding. Before the siding was applied, each board was run through a trough of semi-transparent stain. Any stain puts tension on the finished side; staining all four sides prevents cupping. The golden siding was paired with brown siding that runs horizontally on the house; red-stained siding runs above the entrance to the cottage and *storehaus*. ■

PART FOUR

The *claddagh* symbol on the front door knocker of the Nordgren house shows a heart, a crown, and two clasped hands,

THE HOUSE hailing all who cross the threshold with greetings of love, loyalty, and friendship. The souvenir may be Irish, but the covered entryway is thoroughly Swedish, with benches for an exercise that's universal in muddy climes—taking off your boots! Loren Nordgren enjoys bringing people into the main house

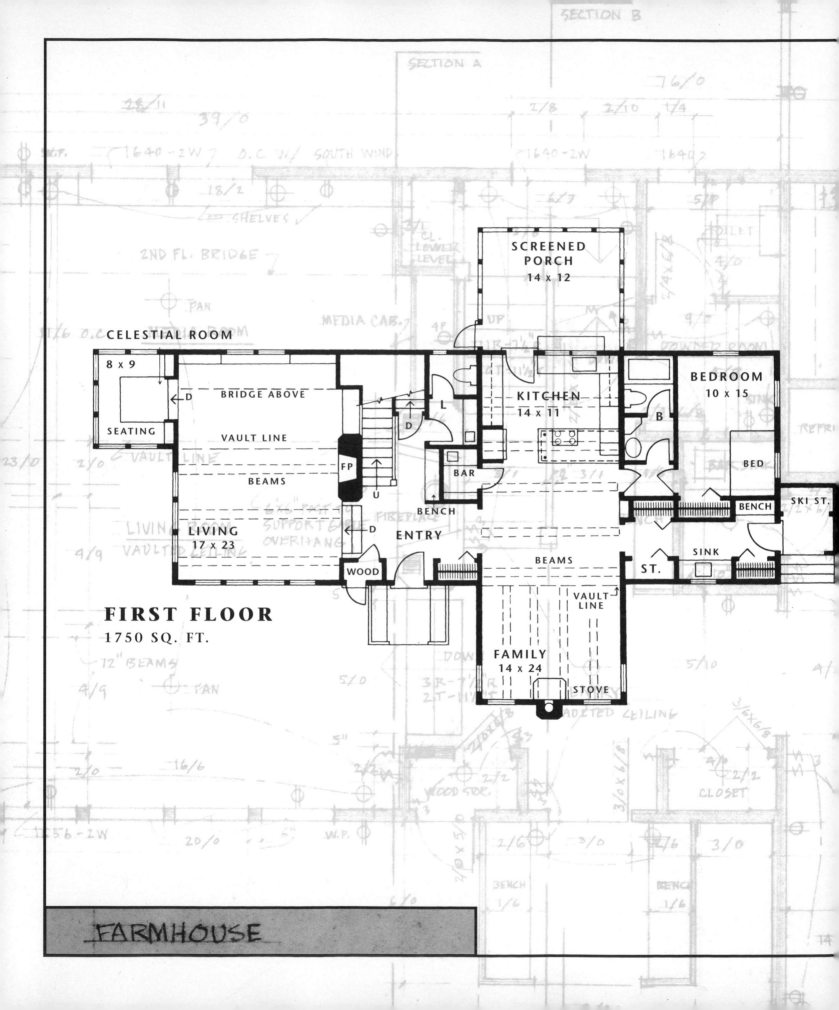

CELESTIAL ROOM

8 x 9

SEATING

BRIDGE ABOVE

VAULT LINE

BEAMS

FP

D

LIVING
17 x 23

ENTRY

WOOD

D

U

L

D

BAR

BENCH

SCREENED
PORCH
14 x 12

UP

KITCHEN
14 x 11

B

BEDROOM
10 x 15

BED

BENCH

SKI ST.

SINK

ST.

BEAMS

VAULT
LINE

FAMILY
14 x 24

STOVE

FIRST FLOOR
1750 SQ. FT.

FARMHOUSE

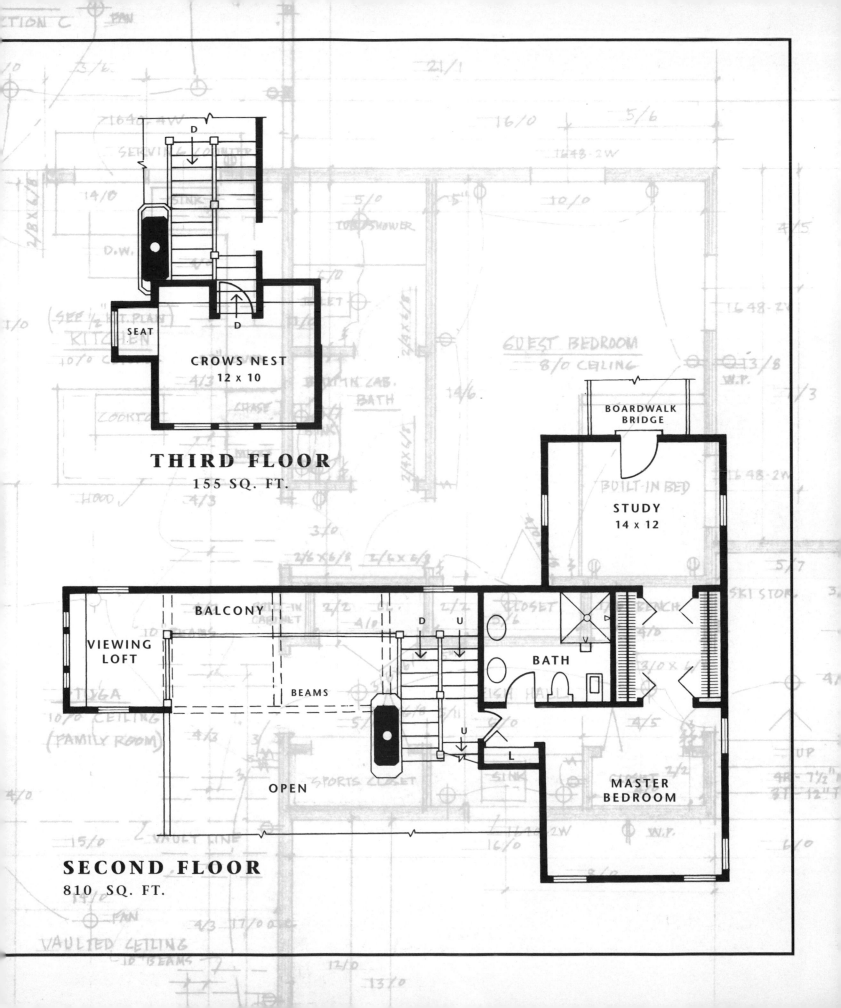

CROWS NEST
12 x 10

SEAT

THIRD FLOOR
155 SQ. FT.

BOARDWALK
BRIDGE

BUILT-IN BED

STUDY
14 x 12

BALCONY

**VIEWING
LOFT**

BEAMS

D   U

CLOSET

BATH

SKI STOR.

OPEN

SPORTS CLOSET

U

L

SINK

**MASTER
BEDROOM**

SECOND FLOOR
810 SQ. FT.

for the thrill of throwing open the door to his special closet. "I'll say to a visitor, 'Open that door,' and they expect to see coats. Instead, they find a pile of wood eight feet high!" This is just one of the many surprises in the carefully conceived lay-out of the Nordgren homestead.

Most houses are built, then decorated. With this house, both things happened at once. From the beginning the plans called for large, open spaces balanced by cozy, more intimate hideaways, like the celestial room emblazoned with a starry ceiling, and the second-floor loft with a view of the lake. An imposing fireplace in the living room and a

Swedish tiled stove in the family room set the stage for family get-togethers.

Heiser laid out a soft Gustavian color palette for the living room, adopting the pale, cool tones

Building a fire doesn't require a trip outside for wood, thanks to the log closet (above), an inge-niously designed holding area between woodpile and fireplace. Logs are loaded into the closet from outdoors; the insulated exterior door keeps out the cold. Decorated paneled doors are seen all over Scandinavia. Mount-ing a horseshoe on the door is an idea borrowed from the Carl Lars-son house. To find the equine footwear, Heiser put out a call to the crew; the next morning, builder Ron Mommaerts brought in a selection of horseshoes, and the door was ready to be shod.

Do you love Life? Then do not squander Time, For that's the stuff Life is made of.

Painted canvases are mounted over two doorways in the family room, depicting folk scenes in a typically Swedish painting style. Two vineyard workers have come to share their harvest with the lord of the manor (above) in a citified version of a medieval woodcut taken from the popular *Gustavus Adolphus Bible* of 1618; the scene may also be interpreted as a friendly interchange between Loran Nordgren and some of the people who worked on the house.

of Swedish palaces. Exuberant primary tones, more Norwegian in feeling, were reserved for the compound's casual family cottage. Interior details sprang from renderings to reality: transom windows and narrow beaded paneling; shelves in every room; lanterns and sconces as primary light sources; and uplifting scenes and phrases painted

Anno 1786

Love One Another Children,
For Love is All.

on canvases mounted on the walls. Surely this would be a place of comfort and delight.

Nordgren loved the tile stoves he'd seen all over Sweden, and ordered one for his family room. Because the stoves weigh 3,400 pounds and require a foundation, Heiser planned for one from the start. It took two men two days to put it together.

The wedding *tapeter* (above) is based on the biblical feast at Cana in Galilee, foretelling future feasts at the Nordgren house. The phrase underneath appears on the wall in Carl Larsson's home. The family room (overleaf) is filled with light from corner windows. Raising the tiled stove on legs brought the fire-box to a better height. Nordgren offspring are named in 10-inch letters on the walls. A trundle bed is hidden beneath the seat of the circa 1700s bench.

THE SWEDISH STOVE

The invention of the heat-retaining Swedish tiled stove was spurred by environmental concerns. Until the 18th century, trees had been cut and burned for fuel in open hearths or in primitive iron stoves. As a result, Scandinavia was plagued by air pollution.

In 1767, the Swedish king proposed a novel idea to inspire the people to find a solution to the pollution problem. He sponsored a competition, offering a prize to whoever could invent the most efficient stove. The prize-winners were ultimately responsible for ushering in a new chapter of Swedish family life. No longer would furniture have to be arranged around the fireplace for warmth. Suddenly new designs were possible and, with that, new and different furniture would be purchased. Dwellings became larger, and doors between rooms were opened, greatly increasing the available living space.

Not surprisingly, since its invention, the tiled stove has held a place of honor in Scandinavian homes. It has become a focal point, dressed with tiles that are either monochromatic or emblazoned with colorful designs. In the Carl Larsson house, one stove's floral tile pattern was echoed on the ceiling in paint. To achieve proper balance in a room, sometimes a cupboard was built opposite a corner stove and painted to match.

The stove in the Nordgren family room is not much different from the prize-winning *kakelungen*, or glazed ceramic tile stoves, invented two centuries ago. A fire started in the morning, inside a very small firebox, will burn for several hours. The smoke travels up and down through flueways inside the chimney, warming the stove's interior heat-storage bricks and its outer ceramic shell. The stove becomes warm to the touch, like a radiator, and keeps the room warm for many hours after the fire has gone out. Another fire is started before bedtime to keep the house warm all night.

In Minneapolis, fine examples of tile stoves can be seen at The American Swedish Institute. ■

Its glossy good looks and promise of warmth make it the focal point of the room.

Peeled pine logs cross the ceiling in the open-plan family room. To decrease their weight, the logs spent two months air drying, and another month in a garage-like kiln, before being bolted in place through blocking in the floor joists overhead. Heiser had seen similar logs on a ceiling in Arizona and climbed up with his tapemeasure to gauge their diameter, so he knew 10- to 12-inch diameter logs were appropriate for this space. With perspective working in his favor, Heiser placed the logs' thinner ends towards the entrance, so that they appear to be uniform.

The house is a brilliant mix of forward thinking and respect for the past. Two hundred years ago, walls were rough textured. To duplicate that rustic look in the Nordgren house, drywall compound was troweled onto taped wallboard, leaving some places bare, before flat paint was rolled on. The ceilings were spray painted. Unstained planks of basswood, 5, 7, and 9 inches wide, were laid on the floors. Basswood is too soft to be a popular flooring today, but was commonly used in the early days of this country because soft woods were easier to saw than hard-

Family room walls (opposite) are solid wood, each vertical board finely edged with a bead and a groove. Many early Scandinavian homes didn't have closets; instead, a room might be ringed with storage trunks like the ones stacked between these Gustavian side chairs. The lap desk's 1843 date shows when it was decorated, not when it was made. Defining the kitchen area (above) is a decorative hood edged with egg-and-dart plaster ornamentation. The hood is partially supported by a pair of twisted iron bars (overleaf). Instead of a toe kick below the cupboards, the cherry countertop extends two inches beyond the cabinets, held up with tiny cherry brackets.

woods such as oak. "My favorite part of the house is the floors," confesses Nordgren. "Wherever you look, you see wonderful knots, rings of growth, and various shades of color."

Old and new is echoed in the traditional Scandinavian layout of an open-plan family room that flows directly into a kitchen-dining area. The ceiling timbers change direction between the family room and the kitchen–dining area, following the lines of the structural purlin beams that support the rafters of the roof. The kitchen is outfitted with the finest equipment, but the floor plan is purposely old-fashioned: a sink on one wall, a stove on the other. The tiled cooking peninsula, topped by an oversized bisque hood, defines the kitchen area without inter-

fering with conversation from the dining area and family room. Opposite the U-shaped work space is a pantry-like storage area with a refrigerator at one end; enclosing the far side of the refrigerator with a wall made it less obtrusive. Cherry shelves were built above for extra storage. The cabinets are custom-

Old-fashioned pantry cupboards were the model for the storage wall (opposite). Glass doors show off fancy china while wooden doors hide everyday pantry goods. Under-cabinet lights illuminate the tiled niche and countertop. The door's heart and circle cutouts repeat the compound's recurring design motif.

Incandescent bulbs hidden above the cupboards reflect light off the white ceiling and bounce it around the room. Cherry shelves in the bake cupboard (above) embrace a line-up of shapely pottery, including hand-glazed polka-dot jasper pots, and a cobalt-blue bowl and pitchers that match the cooktop tiles.

designed so that they appear as if they are an eclectic assortment of furniture; glass doors and open shelving provide areas for display.

Many of the details in the living room were adapted from Carl Larsson's house, including the shed roof and bow and swag stenciling. Transom windows, with removable arching grilles, mimic leaded windows in the Larsson workshop and dining room. Casement windows below are framed with tissue-linen curtains on narrow black iron rods chosen to match the grilles. The room has a wonderful openness and sense of height, just as Nordgren requested.

Engineered to work efficiently, and light enough to be installed without a foundation, the living room fireplace has all the beauty of a masonry fireplace, with none of the complications. Heiser designed a drywall-over-plywood chimney-surround for the prefabricated firebox, and gave it the angular boxed-look of a European stove, like the one in the family room, by covering the lower part with white tile and chamfering the edges at a 45 degree angle. The upper half was decorated in a simple style after dividing it, Carl Larsson–style, into manageable sections using tile braids, an arched recess, and decorative moldings.

The living room, complete with balcony (opposite), sparkles with light. Its tasteful palette of soft blues and greens is typical of late 18th-century Swedish interiors. Furniture arranged in two distinct islands gives the large room a feeling of intimacy. With its decorative swags and pale finish, the Italian commode (above and opposite) sits happily with graceful Gustavian side chairs and the Swedish painted hutch. Stenciling over the windows (overleaf) matches that in Karin's bedroom. Moldings and color organize vertical surfaces into smaller, more manageable "canvases." The lamp in the foyer is four feet tall, but the scale of the space is large enough to accommodate it. Brown paint gave the plaster wall mural a lovely aged appearance.

The house is heated and cooled by a sophisticated ground-water heat pump. Low-voltage circuitry simplifies the wiring, allowing many different lights to be controlled from any room in the house. Music is everywhere, emanating from a surround-sound home-theatre system based in the living room's media cabinet. Speakers and volume controls are built into the walls. There is also a non-directional speaker hidden in the living room floor behind a decorative grille, like the ones that disguise the heat registers. The media cabinet is cooled by natural air flow that drafts through openings in the carved doors, holes in the back of the cabinet, and through the basement below, where additional sound equipment is stored.

Just off the living room is the dramatic sunken celestial room with its spectacular painted ceiling. This is Nordgren's favorite room, one of the brightest in the house. Instead of furniture in this 8 x 9 foot space, a wraparound banquette was built to hug the walls and provide seating for star gazers. The banquette has a practical purpose, too. It hides the foundation, which is exposed due to this room's lower elevation.

The front wall of the living room (opposite) is a symmetrical arrangement of open shelves and bookcases, fenced with moldings and glazed composition rosettes. A band of mannered stenciling decorates the top of the wall. In Scandinavia, light curtains are commonly anchored by fabric rosettes. The antique Baroque faux-stone game table (above), like a gate-leg table, has a top that tilts and hugs the wall when it is not in use. From here, it's two steps down to the sunny celestial room, where the painted ceiling glows with an updated version of the ancient heavens.

CELESTIAL CEILING

"This is Lou Heiser's brilliant idea," says Nordgren, pointing skyward. "I wanted clouds on the ceiling, but Lou took it a step further, creating not just the clouds, but the heavens. The whole room came alive."

Just off the living room is a window-lined nook with a painted celestial ceiling. Heiser had seen a similar room in a Scandinavian book; it had a blue ceiling dappled with five-pointed stars, but he wanted more. Research led him to Alan Lightman's book, *Ancient Light* (1990), which contains Thomas Digge's 1576 drawing, "A Perfect Description of the Celestial Orbes," which became the basis of the pattern for the Nordgren ceiling. Only seven planets were known in 1576, but the Nordgren ceiling shows all nine planets, reflecting the heavens of today.

Painting the ceiling required ingenuity and dexterity—and later, the ministrations of a chiropractor! Bridget Gallagher painted the blue background first, lightly ragging it with white for a Milky Way effect. Then, using a flat piece of wood drilled with holes as a compass, the orbits were drawn with thick lines using a gold paint pen, so that they can be easily seen from below. The compass was temporarily anchored with a screw, allowing it to rotate. The central sun, planets, and astrological signs were all drawn freehand and were individually detailed to distinguish one from another. A simple antique typeface was chosen for the Early English words, duplicating the original drawing. The stars were stenciled using the gold paint pen. Selected stars were highlighted in shades of bright yellow.

A few inches below the ceiling, a coffer circles the room, edged with wide crown molding. The ceiling is uplit by fluorescent tubes hidden in the coffer, giving an eerie cool-blue light to the ceiling at night.

To vent the hidden halogen downlights, a swag effect was created above each window by drilling holes of graduated sizes. The swags not only allow heat to escape from the halogen downlights, but are illuminated by them as well, creating a striking effect; brightened or dimmed at night, they add a certain poetry to the room. Black paint sprayed behind the cornices ensures that even the tiniest holes are visible when viewed from any angle. ∎

Parts of the house look deceptively simple, but had to be planned far in advance. For instance, all the lanterns that seem to be sitting in shelves are actually wall-hung, so electrical boxes had to be positioned and installed in the proper spots long before the walls were built.

Rather than building a framed wall four inches thick around the stairs and the balcony, Heiser opted for a thin, solid stair raising just an inch and a half thick, made from ¾-inch tongue-and-groove boards glued back to back. The wall is locked against the stringer boards of the stairs and vertical posts in the balcony wall. The boards are strengthened by a painted piece of oak that is topped with cap molding, white-painted poplar with half-circle cut-outs that repeat throughout the house, and a handsome cherry railing.

Windows beneath the balcony were installed higher than usual to line up with the bookcases and offer a view of the natural stone wall outside. The balcony itself, which opens to a viewing loft, seems to defy gravity. Hanging off the side wall in the living room, it's actually supported by heavy timbers and plywood bracing.

When it was time to design a newel post for the staircase (above), Heiser remembered a snapshot taken at a historic Wisconsin home. Old Scandinavian farmsteads didn't have media cabinets, but the one by the living room fireplace (opposite) looks as though it might have been carved and painted by artisans long ago. In truth, the handcarved acanthus panels were set into the doors, and then the newly-built piece was painted. The panels have ventilation holes, and lower doors open and slide out of sight to bring the television into full view.

TRADITIONS IN CARVING

The Nordgren farmstead shows examples of dragon-style carving and acanthus baroque carving, two of the many traditional woodcarving styles practiced for centuries in Norway and Sweden. Wisconsin carvers Ann Stakston and Becky Lusk made acanthus panels for the living room's media cabinet, an acanthus-scroll carving for the entrance to one of the built-in beds in the cottage, and eagle and dragon roof ornaments for the house and cottage.

Greek motifs such as the acanthus appear in art throughout the world. This swirling, leafy motif modeled after the native Mediterranean acanthus plant is a familiar adornment on the capitals, or upper portions, of Corinthian columns. The acanthus motif gained particular favor in Norway and Sweden during the mid-17th-century Baroque period. Woodcarvers mimicked the plant's bulbous below-ground root and large thistle-like foliage with their C- and S-shaped scrolls. Swedish acanthus carvings have thin, delicate leaves, like those which crown a built-in bed cornice in the Nordgren cottage; the swirling scrolls that drop down on each side represent the acanthus roots.

Norwegian carving is more robust, exemplified by the media cabinet's acanthus panels edged with a rope-like detail.

English gargoyles have their Scandinavian counterparts in the dragon-style animal shapes adorning the roofs of stave, or vertical post, churches dating from the 12th century. Even as Christianity spread, many people still clung to the past, believing that Norse mythology and dragon heads held more power than Christian symbols.

The Nordgren roof decorations were made by joining basswood boards, using glue and wooden discs called biscuits that fit into side slots in each board, serving as a bridge. Other details—like dragon eyes and eagle wings—are layered on top to form the high points of the design. Soft basswood is easy to carve; it also holds detail well. In order to achieve a clean, sharp cut, the edges of the chisel are fine-tuned every half hour.

Ann is the first woodcarver in her Norwegian family, but other woodcarvers learned their craft from older relatives. Becky Lusk's Norwegian grandfather was a carver, and so are her two uncles. ∎

The viewing loft (above and opposite) forms an L at the end of the second-floor balcony. Halogen floodlights fitted with dimmer-switches are recessed in the ceiling to light the walls. The loft is filled with special details, such as window moldings with a thick key at the top. The illusionist painting on the ceiling harkens back to festival times in Sweden, when a barn's crown rails and ridge poles were festooned with colorful swags and flowers. High-set windows are positioned to take advantage of distant views; after the leaves fall from the trees, the 30-acre lake comes into view.

Instead of a large master bedroom suite, Nordgren asked for a bedroom and separate study, and a bed, just like Carl Larsson's, set in the middle of the room. Heiser duplicated the bed, right down to the brass hooks along the back where clothing hangs. He gave the bed some updates, however; a phone, and a control panel behind the pillows regulate music and indoor and outdoor lights. A built-in television positioned high in the wall borrows space from the cedar closet abutting the bedroom. A 1930s book on English cottages inspired the barrel-vaulted ceilings in the master bedroom and bathroom; only later did Heiser discover the same curved ceilings in pictures of the Larsson house.

There are four windows in the bedroom, and Heiser's original renderings indicated painted details below each one. Sandra Russell advanced this concept and brought it to fruition by devising a story-like succession of paintings about the house, which she painted on canvas *tapeter* and applied to the walls.

Cedar closets line both sides of the commodious three-foot-wide hallway between the master bedroom and neighboring study, and were specifically requested by Nordgren. Their sweet, clean fragrance reminds him of his grandmother's pleasant scent when he was a boy—"a good version of mothballs," he recalls. The saying above the closets is one of Nordgren's favorites, and fits with his philosophy of making the most of every moment. Full-size doors, hinged to fold in pairs, are sturdier than traditional one-inch-thick bi-fold doors. The freestanding bed in the center of the bedroom (opposite) is just like artist Carl Larsson's.

,Sandra Russell painted bouquets on the master bedroom walls (opposite), adding swags, borders, wainscoting, and colorful canvas *tapeter*, mounted below corner windows. These canvases feature oversized squash blossoms, or *kurbits*, and tell traditional tales in a friendly narrative form, interweaving stories about this house with Biblical tales and scenes of life long ago. Inspired by a *tapeter* painted in the early 1800s (above left), this *tapeter* shows workers tending the *kurbits*, alluding to the people who worked on the house. Two men converse (above right); written below in Swedish are their words, "Would you like to ride my horse?" A man rides up to the finished house (below left). The final *tapeter* shows the view from the front door (below right), with everyone relaxing and fishing in the pond.

A trip to St. Bart's inspired an open-plan bathroom instead of the glass-enclosed shower originally intended. Three of the five shower-heads are mounted on the cherry-capped free-standing shower tower (above right) with plumbing concealed inside. The floor tapers to the drain; quarter-inch mosaic tiles are small and thin enough to accommodate the slope. Beneath the tiles, and running a foot up the walls, a leak-proof rubber membrane guards against floods. Heiser made examples of various tile combinations for the walls before settling on this design, with its vaguely Moorish look. Each of the two sinks has a tiled recess behind it, just at sink height, providing storage (opposite). The mirror is mounted flush with the tiles; in lieu of a medicine cabinet, a cherry cupboard sits between the sinks. Across the hall is a commodious linen closet (far left), the lowest shelf elevated to make room for a structural beam.

One of the strong points of the house is its link to the outdoors. Heiser wanted to capitalize on the porch-like aspects of the second-floor study, and knew as soon as the house was sited that he would connect this room to the hillside out back. Contemplating the slope of the land, he came up with a design for a 16-foot boardwalk bridge bordered by crisp white railings, leading from the back door of the study. The bridge is made of weatherized wood and is hinged to the house on pivot heads so that it can float up or down in any weather without breaking away.

Painted on the walls throughout the house are many wise maxims collected by Nordgren, which give the rooms a playfulness. The phrase on the study walls might be the leitmotif of the complex.

"To be of use in this world is the only way to be happy." ■

With gingerbread over the door, a stairstep motif on the gable wall, and latticework below the window, the second-floor study (left) has all the trappings of a little outdoor house. Heiser saw the stepped design on a barn years ago and never forgot it. Nordgren is restoring the chimes to the old Mora clock on the far wall. Outside the door, a boardwalk bridge connects the house to the hillside where Nordgren's trio of flags flies high.

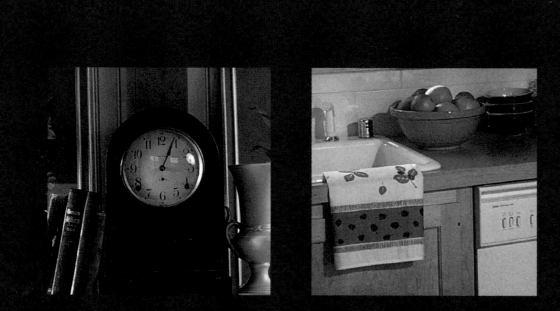

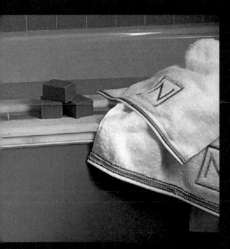

PART FIVE

The cottage has a small footprint but packs a lot of living into 1200 square feet. Designed for the Nordgren children and **THE COTTAGE** grandchildren, it's just a hop, skip, and a jump from the main house, and has a casual, comfortable air. By day, friends and family dangle fishing poles at the pond, and at night, they clamber to claim the built-in beds tucked beneath the rafters and gaze out at the stars. If the accent in the main

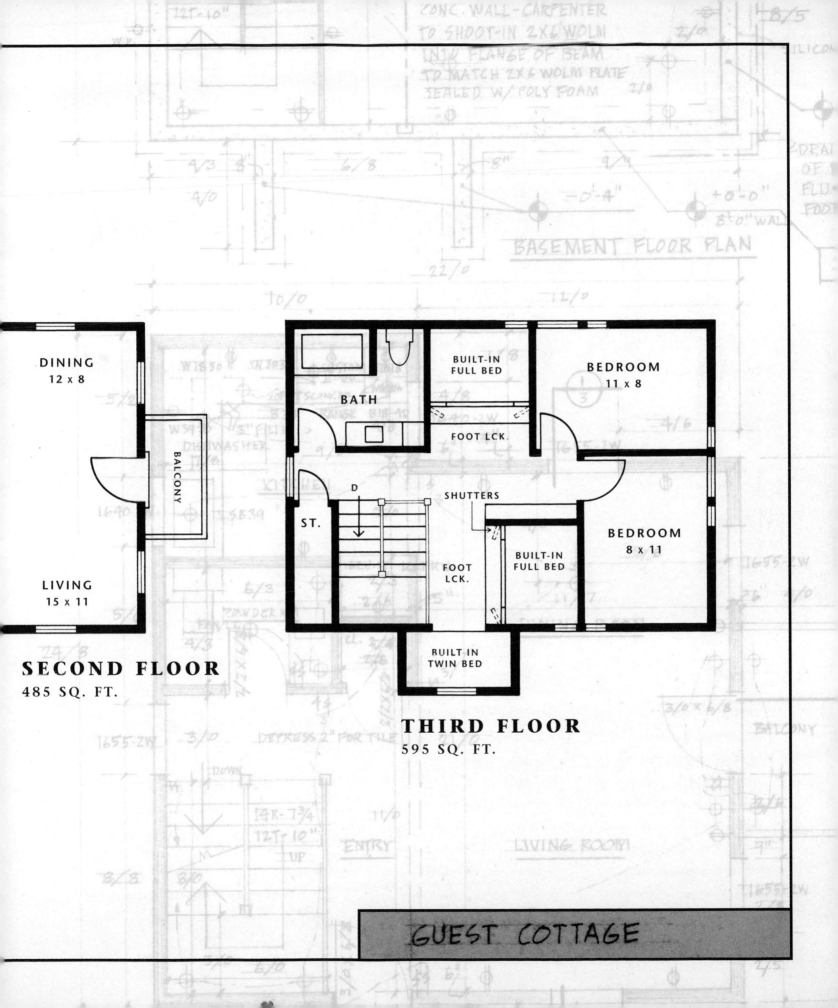

SECOND FLOOR
485 SQ. FT.

THIRD FLOOR
595 SQ. FT.

GUEST COTTAGE

In the cottage, the living is easy. Indestructible machine-washable white denim slipcovers protect the chairs and sofa, which float like pools of ice in a sea of colorful quilts and Swedish-check pillows (above). The foyer table (opposite) is set with vintage accessories, with gardening gear stowed below. Small details count: the door locks and switch plates weren't forged on an old Scandinavian farm, but look as though they might have been. A book on old Scandinavian homes netted the design for the painted frieze ringing the ceiling (overleaf). Fanciful moldings around doors and windows give the cottage its porch-like aspect.

house is Swedish, the cottage is Norwegian: colorful, compact, casual, and designed to handle a crowd. Cheerful primary tones reign here, brilliantly contrasted with yellow and white. Heiser took advantage of the patterns and texture of wooden boards and narrow beaded paneling to repeat a subtle striped effect on the walls. Dark reddish-brown walls in the living and dining area are edged with wavy-cut green window trim. Throughout the

cottage, sections of wall are sharply defined by green moldings.

The small stature of the Nordgren cottage can be deceptive. Built on a hill, it reveals two levels in front, but a lower level at the back adds another big room and bathroom to the mix. Two balconies afford expansive views of the peaceful countryside: a large lower-level balcony, edged with curved white railings modeled after those outside Carl Larsson's house, and a smaller lookout that opens off the living-dining area through a single French door.

The kitchen is as efficient as a pilot's cockpit—small, but powerful enough to pump out meals for a crowd. Heiser chose laminate countertops and hard maple cabinets with a natural finish because he knew they'd be easy to maintain. There are windows on both the south and north sides of the kitchen, so this

In the pirouette kitchen (left), everything is just an arm's reach away. The refrigerator is out of sight, built into the wall opposite the stove. Sconces mounted high on the face of the cabinetry reflect light off the ceiling, and under-cabinet lights illuminate the countertops, eliminating the need for harsh overhead lights. To ensure flowers in the house year-round, china plates decorate the walls. Sandra Russell painted a spirited floral motif over the stove after mapping out the design in chalk.

With such a large family, Nordgren's decision to build a separate house for the children and grandchildren was rooted in practicality: after a certain hour, everyone is happy to retreat to their own quarters. And what delightful places to sleep! On the second floor of the cottage is a trio of cozy built-in beds—two full-size, and one twin—decorated inside and out with painted embellishments that give them a storybook feeling. These beds recall Scandinavian bed cupboards, which were separate pieces of furniture, or sometimes just an alcove in a one-room cabin, curtained off for warmth. The beds are hideaways for reading, sleeping, and daydreaming, and the carpenters used Heiser's kraft-paper templates as patterns to cut the scalloped cornice boards around each one. The panels around the blue bed are hinged so it's easier to make the bed. The yellow bed is decorated with a carved acanthus motif, and the green bed shows horsemen flanking the commemorative date when the house was completed. There are two conventional bedrooms upstairs as well, but, to save space, neither room has a closet because no one lives in the cottage—they just visit. Instead, hanging rods and dressers accommodate clothes, the built-in beds have "footlocker" steps, and there's a narrow storage area for suitcases opposite the bathroom.

Because the upper level of the cottage has so many roof angles, Nordgren encouraged putting the dead space overhead to good use. Heiser devised a pair of house-shaped nooks that delight the eye. Square wood molding became the universal trim upstairs, easily cut and butted into angled corners, and sometimes layered for a stepped effect along the edge of a wall or in corners.

The upstairs bathroom has a lively contemporary look, with a wooden floor and painted wood walls. The tub claims its own private decorative enclosure, framed with the same fanciful carved corniceboards that decorate the built-in beds. Tiles laid in panels give the impression of graphic, colorful Swedish rugs. ∎

Built-in beds, so common in Scandinavia, are undeniably charming. They are also space-savers in the compact cottage (opposite). The vernacular of the multi-peaked roofline is repeated in the bed compartments' sloping roofs and peaked trim. Two witty nooks shelter a pair of birdhouses. Intersecting planes of color are defined by green moldings. A new moon was Bridget Gallagher's serendipitous addition to the twin-bed nook, set in a sky shaded to look like a Maxfield Parrish painting.

Bed-making is a snap because the side panels surrounding the enclosure are hinged for easy access (right). The delicate acanthus shape was carved and applied to the yellow cornice board in two pieces (opposite). The acanthus is one of the most popular motifs in Scandinavian carving, adopted from the Greeks centuries ago. The window, facing west, affords a splendid view of each evening's sunsets. Each built-in bed is outfitted with a window, a shelf, and a low-voltage lantern or sconce for reading.

Two horsemen frame the 1996 bed (opposite), which commemorates the year the compound was completed. The footlocker step contains storage space on either side, but not in the center—so no one falls in! The cottage has fairytale qualities, and many of the walls tell tales, like the mural at the head of the bed. The bathroom tub (left)echoes all the built-in furniture throughout the house. The vanity's laminate countertop, with beveled edge, is hard to distinguish from the genuine cherry shelves in the room.

TRADITIONS IN PAINT

Traditionally, homes in northern Sweden always had a party room, separate from the everyday living quarters, which was used only on special occasions. In this room it was customary—and a sign of family success—to paint murals on all the walls and ceilings. An itinerant painter would paint during the winter, so that come spring, relatives could visit and admire the family's great accomplishments. The more painted surfaces, the more prestige for the owner.

The painting style varied from region to region but the style that became most prominent was *Dalmalning.* The decorative painting that embellishes so many walls and ceilings in the Nordgren farmstead in Wisconsin is artist Sandra Russell's interpretation of *Dalmalning* (also called *Dala* painting).

This style of painting developed in Dalarna, northwest of Stockholm, in the mid-1800s. Artistic young men travelled across the countryside decorating the homes of the common man with details favored by rich townsfolk and royalty, or inspired by the painted interiors of medieval churches. Many of the artists were ex-soldiers and were influenced by what they had seen while traveling with the Swedish army. *Dala* painting often interprets religious stories. History was another popular subject. The artists relied on illustrated Bibles as references, and frequently depicted scenes such as Jonah and the whale, Joseph and his brothers, and the wedding scene in Cana. The lively *kurbit,* the German squash plant, is the central motif of all *Dala* painting.

For the painter, improvisation was often necessary: if an artist had never seen a vineyard, for example, he simply painted what was in his own imagination. Therein lies the charm of *Dala* painting, which is lighthearted, exuberant, and allows for individual expression, unlike rosemaling, which was a more mannered and exacting form of painted decoration of that period. The narratives in *Dala* painting were often personalized with references to the homeowner or current events—sometimes with humorous results.

The scene opposite, painted inside one of the built-in beds in the cottage, depicts a tale of immigration interpreted from a mural at the American Swedish Institute in Minneapolis. ■

PART SIX

The compound was designed in tandem with nature, and nature responded: wild turkeys patrol the grounds daily, while THE OUTDOORS nesting eagles soar overhead. The turf-roofed *storehaus*, garage-gazebo, and entrance porches to the house and cottage, blur the line between indoors and out. Loosely enclosing the quadrangle are rock walls and potted plants that set off the buildings with natural frames. Cheerful colors, metal roofing, and

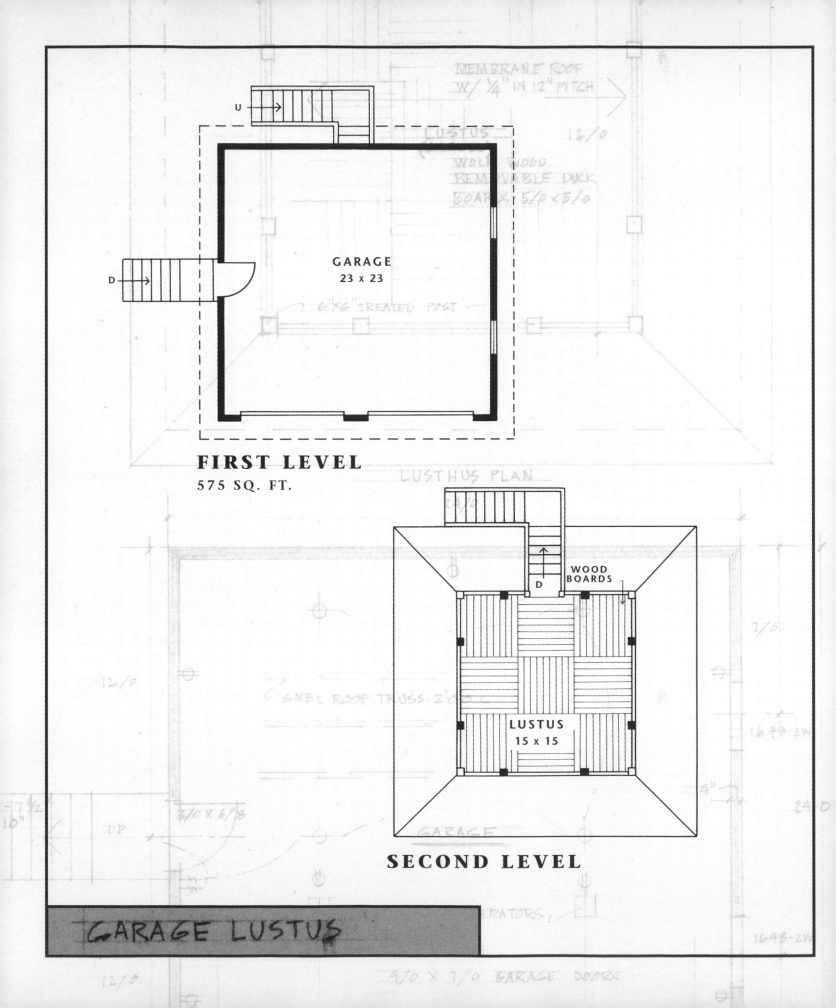

GARAGE
23 x 23

FIRST LEVEL
575 SQ. FT.

U →

D →

WOOD BOARDS

D ↑

LUSTUS
15 x 15

SECOND LEVEL

GARAGE LUSTUS

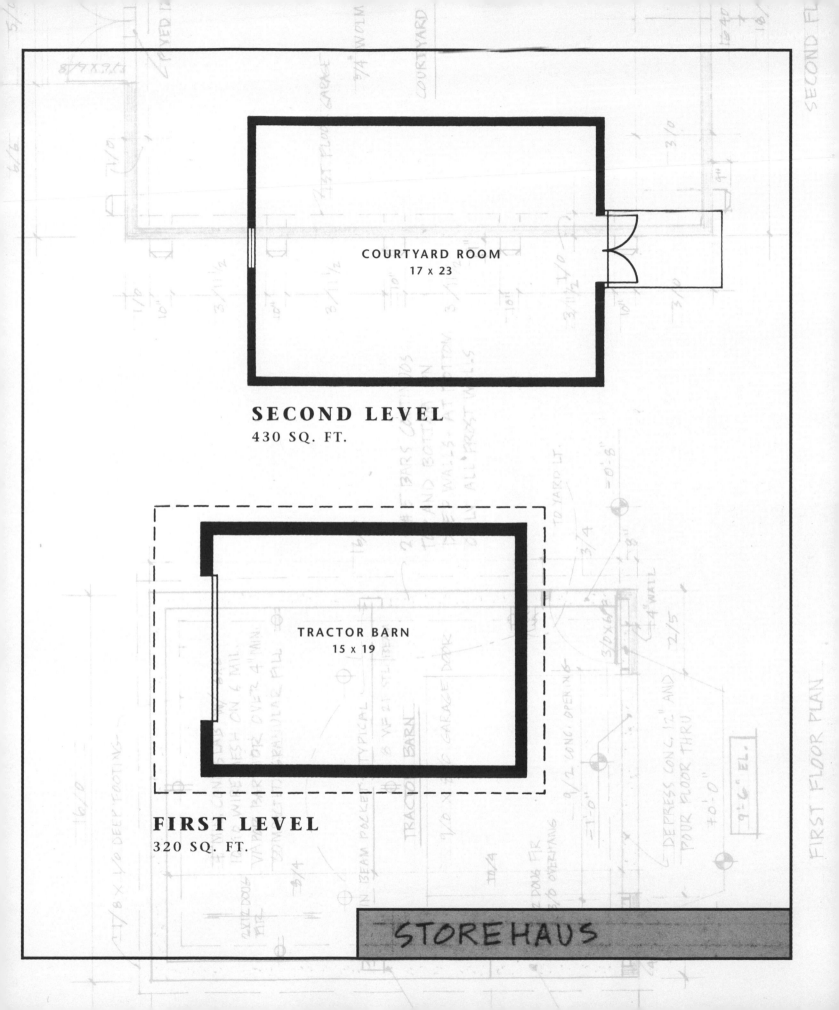

COURTYARD ROOM
17 x 23

SECOND LEVEL
430 SQ. FT.

TRACTOR BARN
15 x 19

FIRST LEVEL
320 SQ. FT.

STOREHAUS

whimsical woodwork brought traditional Swedish character to the farmstead. Heiser was intrigued by the mythical roof decorations on buildings throughout Scandinavia, and designed birds and other beasts for the house and cottage. Nordgren's favorite bird, the eagle, was adopted for the roof peaks of the house—the bird's wing tipped higher and higher as the design evolved to make it look more ferocious—while a traditional Norwegian dragon guards the cottage. To prepare the designs, Heiser used an overhead projector to screen the images onto the wall of his studio. Then he sent a member of the crew up to the roof, with a cardboard silhouette of each carving, to make sure they were the proper size. When he was certain they were just right, he gave the designs to the woodcarvers.

Two other structures surround the central courtyard. The *storehaus*, with its timbered exterior and charming sod roof, looks like an authentic transplant from a remote *coulee* in Norway. Built on a steep-sloping hill, its upper story is accessed from the north, the lower level from the south, where Nordgren keeps his tractor and, formerly, his canoes. The canoes have been moved from the *storehaus* to a mobile canoe house built on a steel

A dragon tail on the cottage and an eagle tail on the house (opposite) bring playful flourishes to the gable ends of both structures. The "carpenter merriment," as the Swedes call it (above), is more than beautiful: it serves as a bridge between two colors of siding laid in different directions. Snowy white boards finish off the corners with a striking brightness.

trailer, which is hauled down to the river during good weather and brought back to the house for storage during colder months. With the canoes gone, the upper level of the *storehaus* is now a party space, decorated in primitive Scandinavian fashion. Log siding covers the walls and the floor is newly painted with exuberant designs. "Several years ago I

saw a wonderful movie, *The Field*, set in western Ireland," relates Nordgren. "There's a memorable scene of a party in a barn, and that's what I envision for the *storehaus*."

Next to the *storehaus* is a two-car garage, capped by a charming gazebo. To keep this aerie firmly anchored, it is braced with metal hurricane clips nailed to the walls, and 6 x 6-inch timbers are bolted into the structure of the garage. A flat surface truss supports the garage roof, and extra trusses hold the gazebo roof, with beams bolted to the trusses. With its panoramic perspective, the gazebo offers spectacular views of the property and the pond—its banks sculpted with a bulldozer—

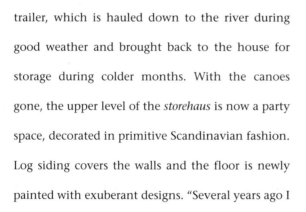

All the exterior trim for these buildings was factory-primed, and required only a final coat of paint. Bright details like the colorful cottage trim (above left) look as lively as Heiser's original drawings. The heart (above right) decorating the rails of the cottage entrance is a Swedish motif with universal appeal. The south side of the cottage (opposite) faces the pond, with balconies off the living room and playroom for taking in the outdoors.

THE SOD ROOF

On a Norwegian farm, animals and tools are traditionally kept in an unheated outbuilding called a *stabur*, or *storehaus*. The *storehaus* is usually made of timbers or rough-cut planks of wood, trimmed with lively painted carvings, and topped by a sod roof laid over protective layers of bark. The slope of the roof is gently pitched to keep the sod from sliding off. The fuzzy grass is often a meal for a grazing goat, and gives a *stabur* an approachable, friendly air. Turf is cheap, readily available, and provides insulation during hot summers and chilling winters. The weight of a sod roof also helps hold a log building together, so it requires less chinking.

Nordgren wanted a sod-roofed *storehaus* just like the ones that nestle in the valleys of Sweden and Norway. Coincidentally, Heiser saw an article in the local paper about imported Norwegian log homes built in Wisconsin. He was able to buy steel "L" brackets and dimpled black plastic surfacing material from a man who imported two log homes but only put a sod roof on one.

To install a sod roof, the egg-crate-like surfacing material is laid over thick plywood. Then two layers of sod are rolled out, the first layer is laid roots up, the next layer is laid grass-side up. As the lower layer of sod decays, the two root systems bind, forming a thick, plush carpet of green. Treated 2 x 8-inch end boards are placed where gutters would normally be, raised an inch off the roof with the steel brackets. Large rocks and small pieces of gravel along the edge of the roof facilitate drainage.

So far, Nordgren's sod roof has required no maintenance or mowing; it seems to take care of itself. Last fall, Nordgren climbed up on the roof to plant daffodils and crocuses in the five-inch-thick turf; he eagerly awaits their debut next spring. Should Nordgren ever become weary of his sod roof, it can be removed and replaced with a more conventional

was enlarged and deepened. Landscaping that compound was a simple affair, the principle being less is more. "If I put any plantings around a house—and often I don't—I like them to be natural and structural, so they don't fight the architecture," says Heiser. "At the Nordgren house, we did put a few bushes next to the family room because it seemed to need something there; but for the most part the house stands alone, and so does the cottage."

Swedish summers are brief and therefore cherished. If you have a vacation house—almost everyone does—you raise a flag to signal you've arrived. It's much the same in Wisconsin. Nordgren flies the Swedish, Norwegian, and American flags at all times, extending a dramatic welcome. The flags were carefully positioned at the back of the house to take advantage of the sloping site. "You've got to get them up in the sky," counsels Nordgren. "Here in America, we don't know how to fly a flag; we've got short thick flagpoles and great big flags. A flagpole should be very tall—at least 30 feet taller than the peak of the building—and the flag should be proportionate in size." His international array fits the bill.

Two years after breaking ground, the compound

neared completion. Of course, a house is always a work in progress; living inevitably sparks new additions and designs. In an effort to control erosion, trees have been planted on the 110 acres no longer rented to farmers. Nordgren has designated his two-mile stretch of river as a catch-and-release stream, and in order to encourage wild fish to take precedence he no longer stocks brook trout. Nordgren has also begun restoring the riverbanks and building shelters to protect fish from predators. There will also be new tenants in the pond, when the trout are replaced by less demanding bass. There are plans afoot to bring back the prairies around the compound by sowing native grasses, and Nordgren anticipates the return of the savannah sparrow and meadowlark. Several people have expressed interest in the hardwood on

Decorative blue bargeboards trim the sod-roofed *storehaus* (opposite). Timber framing gives the exterior of the *storehaus* a rustic look. Like a stairway to heaven, wooden steps and starry votives on crisp white railings lead the way to a sunset party in the gazebo atop the garage (overleaf). The gazebo floor is made of four pallets, which fit together like puzzle pieces and lift out individually if repairs are needed. The pig weathervane in this picture has since been replaced by an airplane weathervane, given to Nordgren by his children as a recent birthday present.

his property, but Nordgren refuses to cut the trees, so that everything can remain—to the extent that it is possible—the same as it's always been.

Nordgren has many visions for the life lived in this house. Among those visions dance *smorgasbord* tables and midsummer celebrations. In fact, the festivities have already begun. In the fall, several months after the project wound down, Nordgren threw a thank-you party to christen the house and acknowledge the people who had worked there. Everyone came: Heiser, the crew, neighbors, and townspeople all gathered for a day-long party. Several months earlier, Heiser performed his own

time-honored rite of succession, after a design is built and completed, and officially handed the keys over to Nordgren. The two men are still in close touch, as the compound continues to grow and change.

Nordgren says he'll never retire, but looks forward to spending more time in Wisconsin.

At an evening celebration up on the roof (opposite), wine, roses, and a sheer tablecloth create romance. Here, and throughout the compound, structural elements are integrated into the design: instead of trying to hide the metal plates joining the roof's cross members, Heiser painted them black to show them off. At night, the house stands all aglow (above), a fitting expression of the warmth and cheer within.

OUTDOOR ENTERTAINING

As striking as the Nordgren compound is in winter, it really blooms in summer, when activity moves outdoors in response to better weather. Wisconsin summers are brief and all the more welcome for their deep blue skies and lovely fair breezes. Midyear celebrations mirror those on the other side of the world, where the seasons are much the same. Norwegian communities hold festivals on *Syttende Mai*, the 17th of May, to commemorate Constitution Day, when Norway was ceded from Denmark to Sweden and allowed its own constitution. Brass bands and banners mark the day, whether you're celebrating in Oslo or Wisconsin. The Swedish mid-summer celebration on the longest day of the year marks June's summer solstice with festivities similar to our own May Day. Everyone heads outdoors for a weekend filled with merrymaking. Dancing around a maypole festooned with flowers, vines, and garlands, signals that warm weather and light-filled days and nights have once again returned.

In August, all of Sweden gorges on crayfish, with feasts outdoors in the gardens. Shells crackle as bushels of the delicate shellfish are consumed.

Smorgasbord literally means bread and butter,

but Scandinavian feasts are so much more than that. A groaning board of herring, sausage, vegetable salads, smoked eel, lobster, breads, and more offer something for everyone, all washed down with icy beer or a potent *akvavit*.

All these influences come to bear during summer festivities at the Nordgren farmstead. A midday lunch on a blanket beside the pond gives

A COUNTRY PICNIC

Wax Paper–Wrapped Vegetarian Sandwiches
with fresh cut cucumbers, radishes, lettuce, tomatoes, and herbs

■ ■ ■

Home-canned Peaches

■ ■ ■

Fresh Strawberries

■ ■ ■

Cool Lemonade and Iced Tea with Sliced Lemon Wedges

■ ■ ■

Fresh Blueberry Pie

■ ■ ■

Chocolate Chip Cookies

way to lazy naptime. A flat-top basket doubles as a table, filled with wax paper–wrapped sandwiches. Ball jars with handles carry beverages with ease.

At night, there's no better lookout than the gazebo, where votives light the table. Household containers find new uses: wine and beer chill in galvanized buckets of ice and water. Smoked salmon and fresh salads provide an authentic Swedish repast, and the evening ends only after a round of jubilant toasts. *Skol*! ■

— A MIDSUMMER — MENU

Mesclun Salad with Walnut Oil and Raspberry Vinaigrette Dressing
tossed with a fresh assortment of edible flowers

■ ■ ■

Homemade Spinach and Cheese Quiche

■ ■ ■

Steamed Asparagus Tossed in Sweet Butter

■ ■ ■

Smoked Salmon with Fresh Dill and Sliced Lemon Wedges

■ ■ ■

Linguine Tossed with Fresh Cut Tomatoes, Basil, Garlic, and Olive Oil
topped with parmesan cheese and roasted pine nuts

21st-century barnstormer, he toys with the idea of marketing aerial videos of surrounding properties, shot from his new plane, an agile Leza-Lockwood Air-Cam. Just as the Larsson family still uses Lilla Hyttnäs

in Sweden, Nordgren has set up a trust so his children will eventually enjoy this property in perpetuity.

The farmstead is forever imprinted with the work of many hands. Anyone who put a paint-brush to a wall or hammered a nail into wood is remembered here. Working together, the crew formed a close bond. The spirit of those days lives on. Sandra Russell explains, "We often run into each other in the grocery store or on the street. Inevitably, the house comes up in conversation. We use it as our standard of excellence. Someone says, 'You know, the way we did it at the Nordgren house.' Someone says, 'Remember when. . .' " ■

While there's still light in the sky, the gazebo offers scenic views of the sheltering hills surrounding the compound. With different accessories and a farm-party menu, the same rooftop setting takes on a more casual look (above). The Scandinavian supper includes cold poached salmon, edible flowers in a tossed green salad, home-baked pies and breads, and wine and beer cooling in buckets of ice. The family likes to picnic by the pond (opposite), the lucky ones crossing the pond by canoe, while others walk around to meet them with sandwiches and provisions. The handmade cedar canoe with handcarved oars is both beautiful and fast.

A R T I

BECKY LUSK & ANN STAKSTON

LOU HEISER

MATT & JAMIE SCHULTZ, ERIN, BRYAN & CRAIG ERICKSON

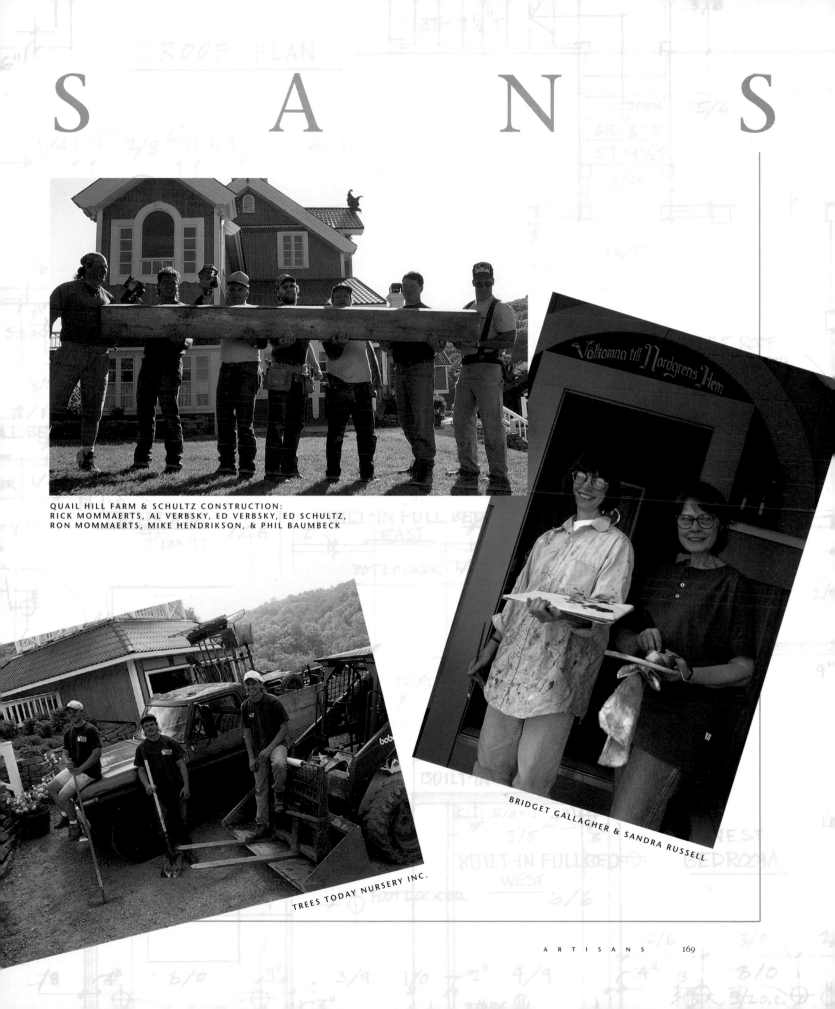

QUAIL HILL FARM & SCHULTZ CONSTRUCTION:
RICK MOMMAERTS, AL VERBSKY, ED VERBSKY, ED SCHULTZ,
RON MOMMAERTS, MIKE HENDRIKSON, & PHIL BAUMBECK

BRIDGET GALLAGHER & SANDRA RUSSELL

TREES TODAY NURSERY INC.

A R T I

COX BUILDERS: FRANK TAYLOR, DAVE ROMARY & CHRIS COX

DAN TAGTMEYER & HARRY ADAMS

TULLY PLUMBING & HEATING

BEAN'S INC.

ELECTRO-FRIDGE

RESOURCE LIST

**PAINTER-
DECORATIVE ARTIST**
Bridget Gallagher
RR 4, Box 350A
Richland Center, WI 53581
(608) 647-7383

WOOD CARVER
Ann Stakston
Rt. 2, Box 90
Cashton, WI 54619
(608) 452-3709

RESIDENTIAL DESIGNER
Tall Tree Studio
Lou Heiser
22001 Ross Road
Richland, WI 53581
(608) 647-2482

DECORATIVE PAINTER
Sandra Russell
Bridget Gallagher
Rt. 2, Box 920
Cazenovia, WI 53924
(608) 647-7351

WOOD CARVER
Becky Lusk
N906 County Rd. PI
Coon Valley, WI 54623
(608) 452-3472

**THE AMERICAN
SWEDISH INSTITUTE**
2600 Park Avenue
Minneapolis, MN 55407
(800) 579-3336

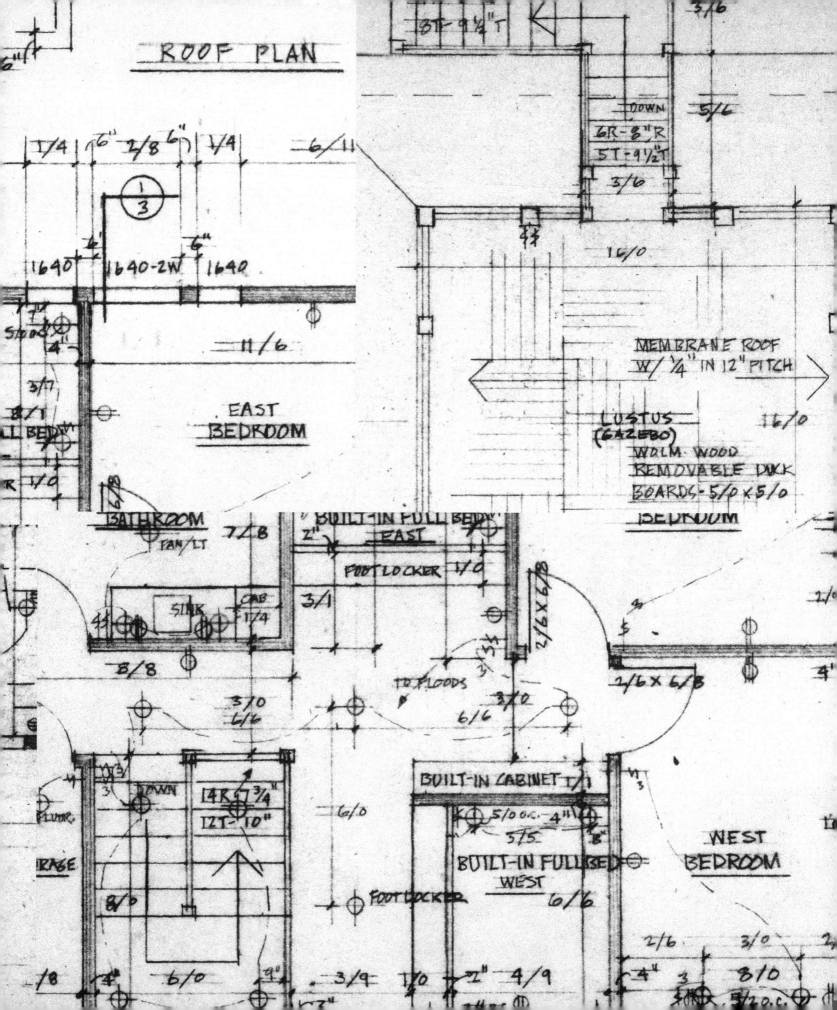

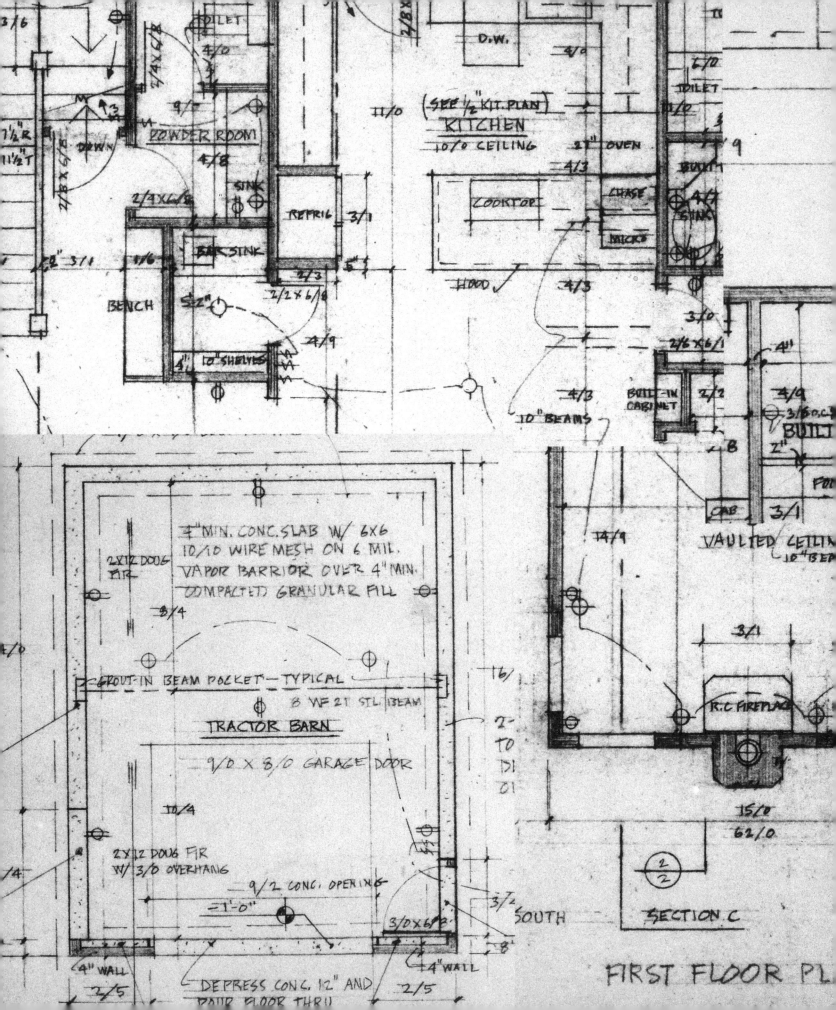

POWDER ROOM

4/8

KITCHEN
(SEE ½" KIT. PLAN)
10/0 CEILING

SINK

REFRIG.

BAR SINK

BENCH

10" SHELVES

COOKTOP

27" OVEN

BUILT

CHASE

MICRO

BUILT-IN CABINET

10" BEAMS

2/6×6/1

VAULTED CEILING
10" BEAM

4" MIN. CONC. SLAB W/ 6×6
10/10 WIRE MESH ON 6 MIL.
VAPOR BARRIER OVER 4" MIN.
COMPACTED GRANULAR FILL

2×12 DOUG FIR

GROUT IN BEAM POCKET — TYPICAL

8 WF 27 STL. BEAM

TRACTOR BARN

9/0 × 8/0 GARAGE DOOR

2×12 DOUG FIR
W/ 3/0 OVERHANG

9/2 CONC. OPENING

=1'-0"

DEPRESS CONC. 12" AND
POUR FLOOR THRU

4" WALL

4" WALL

R.C. FIREPLACE

SOUTH

SECTION C

15/0

62/0

FIRST FLOOR PLAN